UNPICKLED HOLIDAY SURVIVAL GUIDE

JEAN MCCARTHY

Contents

Foreword   v

1. The Most Wonderful Time of the Year?   1
2. Expectations   7
3. The Invites   19
4. Family Gatherings   27
5. Hosting an Event   43
6. Replacement vs. Transfer   55
7. Work Obligations   67
8. Socializing   77
9. A New Tradition   91
10. Your Holiday Toolkit   97

Afterword   109

Foreword

Ah, the holiday season.

So many special events, parties, gatherings, and expectations rolled into a handful of weeks could cause the best of us to feel overwhelmed. For anyone in the midst of making a shift to alcohol-free living, the holidays can be especially tricky. For others who are coasting along nicely in their sobriety, the 'most wonderful time of the year' can also be the most triggering.

Whether you are newly sober, a recovery 'old-timer,' or a supporter of a loved one in recovery, the key to getting from November to January unscathed is to plan ahead by being aware of potential triggers and arming yourself with useful tools and strategies.

This book will help to increase your awareness of possible pitfalls and offer suggestions to avoid them. Each chapter will help you add to your recovery toolkit, and provide suggestions for ways that friends and family can be supportive.

You may decide to read this short guide front to back or hop around as needed, depending on what pops up next on your calendar.

The final chapter (Your Holiday Toolkit) is designed to recap the information shared throughout the book and is laid out as a resource to go.

What does it mean to be sober?

The only assumption I make as write this book is that the reader endeavours to remain alcohol-free. While I do not address recreational drug use in these pages, my personal definition of sobriety is to claim abstinence from both alcohol and drugs. I respect that every person has a right to define and pursue sobriety in their own way. Although the legalization of marijuana will undoubtedly create new social norms, its use (or more pointed, the choice to abstain from use) does not currently seem to carry the same social pressures or assumptions as alcohol consumption.

There are many pathways to recovery.

This book is intended to supplement (not replace) the reader's recovery program(s) of choice. I do not endorse or reject any pathway to recovery.

What is patchwork recovery?

The term 'patchwork recovery' refers to the use of many different tools, program components, and support systems to achieve sobriety and recovery. While many people use well-established, traditional recovery programs successfully, others find success through self-directed means that includes a multitude of philosophies, tools, perspectives, supports, and methods. The patchwork recovery concept embraces the validity of any process that leads successfully to freedom from addiction.

Terms for Alcohol Use Disorder

While the official terminology of the Diagnostic and Statistical Manual of Mental Disorders - Fifth Edition (or DSM-5) uses "Alcohol Use Disorder" as an umbrella term to describe varying degrees of both alcohol dependence and alcohol abuse, this book takes a more conversational approach. In these pages, I use the terms alcoholism, alcohol addiction, alcohol dependency and problematic drinking interchangeably. No specific criteria or diagnosis is implied or intended.

Disclaimer

I am not a medical expert, and the information shared within this book is not intended as medical advice. Please consult physical and mental health professionals for personal assessment and direction.

Still drinking?

You'll find that the information presented in these pages assumes the reader has already embraced sobriety, as this is a guide for *staying* sober over the holidays rather than *getting* sober over the holidays.

Even if you haven't quit drinking yet, you will find this book helpful.

The natural progression of making a change is moving from *contemplation* to *preparation*, followed by *action* and then *maintenance*.

If you are considering sobriety, recovery books like this one will help you transition from the *contemplation* stage of your decision into *preparation*. This is a time of information gathering to arm you with a vision of what to expect in an alcohol-free lifestyle.

Learning more about life after alcohol can help you move from preparation to *action* and eventually change your relationship with alcohol for good.

What about waiting until after the holidays to give up alcohol?

If you feel ready, then the best day to quit is today.

We are conditioned to think of January as a time of new beginnings, so it might be tempting to keep drinking through the holidays and begin sobriety fresh in the new year. The problem with this notion is twofold. First, you may not necessarily feel as ready on January 1st as you are today. And second, if you don't manage to quit that day, it is a whole year before the next New Year's resolution.

There will always be something on the calendar that your addicted brain will suggest ought to be waited out before quitting: a wedding, reunion, or special birthday. It can be a little more challenging to stop drinking during the festive season, but it is possible and worth the effort!

ONE

The Most Wonderful Time of the Year?

But it's a tradition...

Many people find it hard to imagine eggnog without rum or the New Year's Eve without champagne. Alcohol has become synonymous with celebrating. It's a host's duty to keep the glasses full and the guests merry.

Isn't it?

When I quit drinking alcohol in 2011 after more than a decade of daily wine consumption, I trembled at the thought of attending office parties and family gatherings. I'd become conditioned to the use of alcohol as a social crutch and was so out of touch with myself that I'd forgotten how to interact without a stem glass in my hand. My beloved companion.

By the time the festive season rolled around, I was several months sober and had gained some confidence. Even so, the extra demands of the season were tough.

I've since learned that there are many aspects to the festive season that can undermine sobriety. Some sober folks are shocked to find themselves battling cravings and temptations, seemingly out of nowhere, at a family gathering. Others may wish to embark on sobriety, only to find that it feels impossible to navigate all of the social demands that this particular time of year brings.

Thanks to the thousands of comments and messages received via my blog UnPickled, the hundreds of guests I've interviewed on The Bubble Hour podcast, and the many connections I've made online and in-person through recovery groups, the wisdom of others has provided countless lessons and helpful tips.

I assert nothing proprietary about the information shared on these pages. I make no claims as a researcher, expert, or creative thinker, as I consider myself none of these things. My only goal is to share my own experience as a person in recovery and relate the lessons learned from holding space as others tell their stories.

First, let's begin by looking at what it is about this time of year that adds extra pressure to the already challenging task of living life without alcohol.

The cluster of traditional gatherings, holidays and events can result in:

- **Expectations** of ourselves or others that don't turn out as we might hope
- Managing multiple **invitations** that may be overwhelming, especially if we feel obligated to show up at everything
- Spending time with our **family of origin** which forces us back into old unresolved patterns, wounds, or dynamics
- Playing the role of **host**, which may be more stressful than we realize
- **Transfer behaviours** such as shopping or indulging in sweets, which can get out of hand at this time of year
- **Additional work pressures** and commitments
- Playing the role of **guest**, which may be particularly uneasy if we feel pressured to go to events we aren't comfortable attending

Many of these challenges originate in things we consider positive, such as spending time with family or dressing up for a party. It is important to remember that triggers are not necessarily confined to things that upset us. Often the simple disruption of our new sober routines can cause problems.

Permit yourself to look objectively at the traditions you've experienced throughout your life. Consider what aspects of Thanksgiving through New Years (and beyond) may not serve you well, and know that it is okay to do things differently.

No rule says we need to host, or even attend, every family gathering. It is perfectly acceptable to go to bed at 9 p.m. on New Year's Eve. I promise you, the sun will still rise on January 1st, whether you were awake or asleep at midnight.

Perhaps it is time to make some new traditions.

Reflection Exercise:
Spend some quiet time considering how you genuinely feel about the holiday season. What pleases you, and what makes you anxious? What do you look forward to, and what do you dread?

Tool: Willingness
It's essential to be willing to do things differently if you would like to see change. Give yourself permission to question the usual way of doing things and stand by any decisions you make in your own best interest.

Tips for Friends and Family:

Support your loved one in recovery by being open to change. Understand that it can be difficult for them to live life differently if everything around them stays the same. Begin with a private conversation to ask if there is anything special you can do to support their recovery during holiday events. If they share with you that some aspect of the usual tradition is challenging for them, listen without judgement and do not take offence. It is not a criticism of you or the way you do things. Consider new ways of doing things and be willing to compromise.

Wisdom from Sober Friends

" Holidays used to be one big party...lots of drinking. As I was newly sober last year, it was just something to survive and get through sober. This year I'm looking forward to more quality time with family and friends who support my sobriety.

Liz (14 months of sobriety)

" I no longer feel bad for myself for not "getting to drink." I definitely NEEDED to go through a few holidays to build my muscles

Laney (3+ years of sobriety)

" Each year not drinking has gotten easier, and now I enjoy the holiday season more than ever! With no hangover, I don't have to kill myself baking, entertaining, standing on my head....whatever to [overcompensate]. So I just enjoy! The magic of the season isn't over-shadowed by a hangover or obsession with my next glass of wine. My party conversations are more authentic and memorable. Waking up knowing the drunky-pants stories aren't about me puts a big smile on my face.

Marci (1064 days of sobriety)

TWO

Expectations

Expectations are premeditated resentments.

The above statement is an old gem from Alcoholics Anonymous and something worth writing on your palm.

What do you expect?

I used to think that having high expectations for myself and others was a great thing. I offered it up as a positive attribute and one of the secrets to my success back when, you know, I was almost perfect and *killing it* except for my teensy tiny problem of drinking myself to sleep every night.

"I accomplish a lot because I ask a lot of myself," I'd say, and it was true.

What I didn't understand was that I had it all backwards. I thought my expectations were what made me successful.

What I learned in recovery, however, was that one reason I had such high expectations for myself was that I thought less of myself than others. It was hard to see this as low self-esteem because I could intellectualize my worth, but only insofar as I appeared to others.

Since others thought of me favourably, so did I. Therefore, I had no control over my perception of myself.

I thought it necessary to over-achieve to compensate for flaws and faults. I didn't feel safe unless I did more. I didn't feel loveable unless I'd earned some kind of value.

To further add to the confusion, over-achieving is often rewarded personally and professionally. Everyone wants the 'go-getter' on their team, and that feels good to someone who only values herself as seen by others.

The problem is that each of us tucks ourselves into bed at night and turns inward before falling asleep. The world is not there to whisper 'good job' and stroke our foreheads as we drift off. Whether for a few moments or for endless hours of tossing and turning, each of us must eventually come face to face with our own personal truth.

That was the moment I drank to avoid. I hoped to perfectly time my intake so that darkness might fall over my mind a nanosecond before my head hit the pillow.

I became obsessed with bedtime, carrying a last (huge) glass of wine up to the nightstand to usher me into sleep. I'd finish half and return to the kitchen for more, just a wee top up to get the job done.

Heaven forbid it didn't work.

If sleep did not come quickly, I'd soon find myself replaying old memories as evidence of my human failure, a montage of short-comings and missteps. I'd worry about the future and 'terriblize' the past, berating myself while imagining the abandonment I surely deserved. I cried silently for fear of waking my husband, who I was sure would be horrified if only he knew the 'real' me.

I felt captive in my own mind, scared and afraid in the dark. It was a stunning contrast to the life I led by day as a confident, outspoken business owner and industry leader.

This disconnect eventually became unbearable.

It was as though I was wearing a suit of armour, looking strong and large from the outside, but underneath it, I felt shrivelled and weak. The armour became heavier, and I became weaker, less able to hold it up and manipulate it convincingly.

Just three weeks after I quit drinking, I came to realize the importance of freeing myself from this self-created dynamic. I'd written about a complicated exchange with my parents, and a wise, sober reader named Bob S. commented to share the role that expectations play in our troubles: "Expectations f— alcoholics and turn into resentments."

I didn't use meetings to get sober, but I understood Bob S. was referencing an aspect of the Twelve Steps of Alcoholics Anonymous.

Like most people, I had a vague notion that the A.A. process involved making a list of all the bad things ever done and then going out to set them right. My sons used to enjoy a tv show called "My Name is Earl," and we'd laughed together about the antics of this fellow in recovery who went around with a tattered paper trying to correct his mistakes.

I was confused by this notion of repairing wrongs because I hadn't hurt anyone else by drinking myself to sleep at night.

But there is another list that comes earlier in the process, something the program calls a "searching and fearless moral inventory."

Yikes.

Wasn't that what I was doing every night instead of sleeping? Wasn't that what I was drinking to avoid?

The next step is to read that list to another person, a confession of sorts, followed by the willingness to have shortcomings removed.

Online exchanges with others who were working this program for themselves shed further light on the process, and one person revealed that they were reworking this step with a list of resentments. They explained that healed resentments were a key to staying peaceful, which in turn helped them stay sober.

Connecting the dots between expectations and resentments changed my thinking dramatically, and made me hungry to learn more about recovery.

Self-reliance is essential, but it can become exaggerated into isolation and avoidance. I was so proud of my independence and ability to achieve. How could it be a negative thing?

- I expected myself to be self-reliant yet resented others for not helping.
- I expected others to judge me yet resented the feeling of judgement.
- I expected others to care what I thought of them yet resented them for not valuing my opinion by taking my advice.
- I expected to be exposed as unworthy yet resented the fear this caused.
- I expected others to appreciate my achievements yet resented that I never felt truly worthy of praise.
- I expected to feel good when I achieved a goal yet resented feeling pressured to continually achieve more.

As this understanding sank in, I wrote the following on my blog:

> Over the years, my quest for perfection has driven me in so many ways.
> It's the reason I am meticulous with my looks – dressing carefully,
> always made up nicely with hair done well. It's the reason I work out
> daily and know the amount of fat and calories in every different brand
> of yogurt. I've won scholarships…awards, [and] recognitions…
> Is it any wonder that wine flowed through the cracks in the armour?
> All I really want is a gold star for my efforts every day.
> I don't do all these things for my own satisfaction; I do them so others
> will approve. I expect them to approve, and justifiably so.
> But here's the problem: I can't make them…

Holidays come laden with traditions and expectations, making them a breeding ground for resentment.

The fact that so many events are squished into one quarter of the annual calendar further weakens our defences against the possible pitfalls of the festive season.

The way our *families of origin* (see Terms in Chapter 10) celebrated the holidays can set the stage for our expectations, normalizing whatever level of festivity and effort was demonstrated throughout childhood. We carry this idea of "normal" (a word that should forever require scare quotes) into our adult years. Then we work to assimilate "normalcy" into the additional requirements placed on us by external forces like our work cultures, social circles, extended family, and those of others with whom we may share our lives.

Add to this the forces of pop culture, Pinterest suggestions, and mommy blogs about hand-crafted wrapping paper. Christmas movies on the Hallmark channel. Perfect-looking families on social media.

Who needs to think for themselves when we are bombarded with such convincing evidence of what's required for a happy occasion?

What do you consider non-negotiable elements of your traditional occasions? Where do those elements originate, and why do you find them essential? I challenge you to sit with a pen and paper and assess an upcoming event with these criteria. What ideas are genuinely your own, and what are ingrained patterns perpetuated by rote?

If you believe that you *have to* do certain things, you are falling into the trap of expectations and opening yourself up to resentments.

Resentment is discomfort. Unattended discomfort can undermine recovery.

In the hundreds of interviews I've conducted on the Bubble Hour podcast, one consistent reason people give for developing a regular drinking habit has been as a way to cope with discomfort. Some use it to make socializing easier, some as an emotional salve for unhappiness, some drink to self-medicate anxiety, depression or trouble sleeping.

At first, alcohol seems to work as a way to ease problems, which leads to continued and escalated use. Once a physical dependency develops, the drinker can experience discomfort 6-8 hours after the last drink that feels like anxiety or emotional distress but is actually withdrawal. Believing that alcohol is the cure for these feelings, rather than the cause, makes the cycle continue.

Once alcohol use is discontinued, the pattern is disrupted, and new comforts must be sought as replacements.

Physical cravings can diminish within a few days or weeks, but it can take much longer to create new emotional connections to other forms of relief.

To recover is to create a life in which numbing is no longer necessary for survival.

If sobriety is about living alcohol-free, then recovery is about building new patterns and behaviours that make life more comfortable, so we don't need to cope with numbing mechanisms.

New routines must be established, new ways of thinking and interacting. As we recover, we reshape our lives to support this new and better way of doing things.

Then comes the holiday season.

Eeeeerch.

We travel to spend time with family and suddenly realize that the new routine is not as portable as we thought. Or we take it with us when we go, only to find that our needs require some unanticipated accommodation by our hosts that is perhaps unwelcome. Or maybe we just don't feel comfortable speaking up for ourselves, fearing conflict, rejection, or unwanted attention.

This is how I'm spending my vacation? I'd rather be home.

Then it becomes our turn to host, and any self-care regimine goes out the window to make room for 34 dinner guests and an inflatable mattress in the rumpus room.

When will these people leave so I can have some time to myself? I thought it would be over by now.

Assess your expectations.

Expectations can be hard to spot because they are camouflaged by normalization. It can be easier to identify them by considering what we find disappointing.

For example, I'm disappointed when others don't observe common courtesies, such as holding a door for the next person or picking up their dog's poo in the park. Anyone who fails to signal a lane change or leaves their shopping cart uncorralled is clearly a sociopath.

These resentments reveal my expectations.

Is it fair of me to assume that everyone was taught the same rules and manners? Must we all value these things equally?

I've learned something more, something harder to admit. I take things personally and feel slighted when another person demonstrates that they don't care what I think of them, even in small matters of public courtesies. Consequently, I resent the power that other people have to make me feel diminished.

The truth is, sometimes people are rushed or preoccupied and may not even realize someone is behind them. Why should I allow that to deflate me?

My expectations set me up for a discomfort based entirely on perception rather than truth. That's a lot of power to give away.

Here are some common ideas that can become normalized around the holidays:

- I have to visit or host extended family because it is a special family occasion

- I have to follow the family traditions because that is how everyone wants it done
- I need to host an event when it is my turn
- I have to be polite by eating/drinking the fancy things that others put a lot of effort into making, even if I don't want to
- I have to serve alcohol to others because it is festive
- I have a list of people who I need to buy gifts for
- Everyone should like the gift I choose for them or at least appreciate the thought
- I have a good idea of who should be giving gifts to me
- I will receive the gifts that I've been hoping for
- I will probably get things I don't even like and have to pretend I like them
- Big events should be celebrated a certain way
- My house must be decorated
- I have to consider everyone's feelings when I'm making plans

Nothing on this list seems overly dramatic or even out of the ordinary, yet every item can be tested for its truth.

What if we reconsider the list with some adjustments? Try reading it aloud if you're feeling extra brave.

- *I may be expected, by myself or by others,* to visit or host extended family because it is a special family occasion *but it isn't true that I must*
- *I may be expected, by myself or by others,* to follow the family traditions *but it isn't true that I must*
- *I may be expected, by myself or by others,* to host an event when it is my turn *but it isn't true that I must*
- *I may be expected, by myself or by others,* to be polite by eating/drinking the fancy things that others put a lot of effort into making *but it isn't true that I must*
- *I may be expected, by myself or by others,* to serve alcohol to others because it is festive *but it isn't true that I must*

- *I may be expected, by myself or by others,* to buy gifts for others *but it isn't true that I must*
- *I may expect others to* like the gift I choose for them or at least appreciate the thought *but it isn't true that they must*
- *I may have an expectation* of who should be giving gifts to me *but it isn't true that they must*
- *I may have an expectation that* I'll receive the gifts I've been hoping for *but it isn't true that I will*
- *I may have an expectation that* I'll get things I don't even like and have to pretend I like them *but it isn't true that will happen*
- *It may be expected, by myself or by others,* that big events should be celebrated a certain way *but it isn't true that they must*
- *I may be expected, by myself or by others,* to have my house decorated *but it isn't true that I must*
- *I may be expected, by myself or by others,* to consider everyone's feelings when I'm making plans *but it isn't true that I must*

Therapy was worth every penny.

I like to get my money's worth out of therapy by repeating the lessons I've learned for anyone who will listen. Somehow it gives me the feeling of stretching the value.

When newly sober, I noticed that I was emotional after every family gathering at my parents' house. I'd learned about the connection between expectations and resentments, and thought I'd impress my therapist by telling her that my new plan was to expect the worst from family gatherings so that I could avoid disappointment.

She kindly, and wisely, pointed out my logic would then result in disappointment if things went well.

Being too busy bracing ourselves for blows can cause us to miss the positive things that might happen.

"So, what then?" I asked. I was utterly perplexed.

"You take all of the values and standards you've created for your-self," she explained, "and imagine yourself encased in a bubble that keeps these things close to you. You interact with others through this bubble, always honouring the things that are important to you. You focus on your own conduct and only measure the success of the event by how well you were able to stay true to yourself."

She told me that I often mentioned how much I value kindness and loyalty.

"Keep those in your bubble with you. Every exchange you have with family should honour your commitment to kindness and loyalty, even when you disagree. Disagree kindly while staying loyal to yourself and your principles."

Reflection Exercise:
What standards and virtues do you value and wish to practice at all times? What is inside your bubble with you wherever you go? What aspects of your own conduct will you use as a measure of success?

Tool: Discernment
Learn to identify the things you assume are "normal" that are really expectations. Letting go of expectations will reduce negative feelings of resentment that undermine recovery.

Tips for Friends and Family:
Think about the ways that you and your loved one in recovery may hold unspoken expectations for one another regarding holiday events and traditions. Have a discussion to explore these expectations and decide if they are real or perceived, fair and necessary, and consider ways that you can release one another from them. Swap expectations for agreed-upon responsibilities and boundaries for all family members, then be patient as dynamics shift.

Wisdom from Sober Friends

" I no longer hold on to expectations. Living alcohol-free has brought about a shift in how I live my daily life. Quality over quantity. I don't over-schedule. I take care of myself and make sure I'm enjoying each and every day, including the holidays. I measure success by my ability to take in the smallest of moments now. It's as if I needed large, loud, ongoing events as a drinker so it could have an effect on me. My senses now are finely attuned to the simple sounds, smells, sights.

That is a gift in itself.

Diana (25 months of sobriety)

" [I'm] heading into my first alcohol-free holiday season and looking forward to experiencing it through new eyes. My expectations have changed, throughout recovery, in that I am now looking forward to being fully present with family and friends, rather than dreading the idea of "missing out" on my old favourite holiday drinks. This year, I'm mixing and serving a variety of fun alcohol-free drinks along with the festivities.

Kat (157 days of sobriety)

" I keep my expectations in check. I perform a lot of self-care beforehand and plan for treats afterwards.

Elizabeth (23 months of sobriety)

My first sober holidays were awful. I was in a foul mood for a month straight and just did my best to get through them with a fake smile plastered on my face. This year I'm actually excited to participate in traditions that are not alcohol focused, like baking cookies with my daughter. I also try to make sure I'm taking time to focus on my recovery. Usually, this means going back to the basics like listening to extra sobriety podcasts, taking extra baths, and keeping up my attendance at A.A. meetings. I'm also going to buy myself a fun advent calendar this year.

Sarah (500 days of sobriety)

THREE

The Invites

I really can't say no to this event…

Staying true to your recovery pathway can depend greatly on the situations you choose to for yourself.

During the holidays, invitations can feel more like obligations. As the previous chapter on expectations shows, feeling pressure to do things can lead to resentments, which, in turn, dial-up discomfort and undermine our recovery.

Do you want to go?

For every event, during the holidays or otherwise, first assess your interest in attending rather than the idea that others will be disappointed if you don't participate. The question is not "Should I go?" but rather, "Do I want to go?"

Are there particular circumstances to consider?

Is this the year that Cousin Gordon is visiting from abroad? Has the company hired your favourite comedian to headline the annual gala? You may not want to go otherwise, but special circumstances can make the invite worthwhile despite your hesitation. Focus on positive elements that make the event important to *you*. Worrying that family members might be offended by your absence does not count.

Will it be a safe environment for you at this point in your recovery?

Depending on your stage of sobriety, some environments can be uncomfortable and even risky. In early recovery, every situation that includes alcohol can be triggering. As we become more adept at navigating social events over time, it gets easier to look after own needs. Other factors besides exposure to alcohol can be uncomfortable as well, such as returning to a location where a traumatic event occurred or a situation that provokes social anxiety. If you don't feel you will be able to protect your sobriety, do not go.

"No Thank You" is a complete answer.

If you decide against accepting an invitation, a simple "I can't make it but thank you for asking" is all you need to say. Do not make excuses or give explanations, as this will only invite attempted persuasion. If you feel pressured or are made to feel guilty, stand by your decision with kind firmness.

Here are some examples of pressure tactics you may encounter and responses to consider:

WHEN SOMEONE SAYS: "It won't be any fun without you."

Reply: "That's sweet of you to say, but I'm sure you'll all have a great time."

WHEN SOMEONE SAYS: "Mom will be mad if you don't come."

Reply: "I understand. Sorry I can't make it."

. . .

WHEN SOMEONE SAYS: "You have to come. Everyone else will be there."

Reply: "Have fun. We will get everyone together another time."

WHEN SOMEONE SAYS: "Why aren't you coming?"

Reply: "It doesn't work for me this year, but thank you for the invite."

"YES, BUT…" is also an option.

"Yes, but I have to leave by eight."

No one needs to know that the "other event" you're rushing off for is a bubble bath! If the event is away from home and includes spending the night as a guest, arrange for your own lodging nearby.

It's completely honest to tell the host that you have another commitment to attend because self-care is indeed a commitment.

If you choose to attend…

Be prepared.

Bring your own alcohol-free beverages if possible or, if you are at a restaurant or a catered event, speak to a service person about options. (At restaurants, I ask for my wine glasses to be removed and simply drink water. This saves confusion for the servers when they are filling glasses and stops them from continually offering me wine at dinner, which gets tiresome.)

Have your own transportation so you can leave the event when you are ready. My husband and I have left countless parties separately. We agree that I can take the vehicle home when I feel I need to go, and if he isn't ready, he will hire a cab later.

Bring a snack. That's right. Bring a snack, even though there will probably be oodles of food. You may not need it, and it may seem silly but do it anyway. Tuck a little cheese packet or granola bar in your pocket. If the dinner service is delayed or if you're allergic to half the menu, you need to have a solution for one of the most common and least obvious triggers for alcohol cravings: hunger.

Bring a gift to offer the host when greeted. Use this interaction as an opportunity to add quietly, "I may have to slip out early, so don't worry if you notice that I've disappeared. Let me thank you now for having me. I'm looking forward to a great time." This will save you having to track down your hosts to announce your departure, and can also head off any buzz about why you've gone. Then if you do decide to leave the party abruptly, you will have shown thoughtfulness and gratitude to the host in advance.

(Note: many people habitually bring wine as a gift for the host, especially as drinkers themselves. Now that you are a non-drinker, be more inventive. I maintain a stash of candles, pate knives, tea towels, and fancy soaps along with little gift bags and note cards. It's easy to choose something tasteful from the cupboard and dash off a quick note as I'm headed out to an event or gathering.)

Bring someone with you as a backup. If your social circle is not aware that you've quit drinking, then it is helpful to have one trusted person who can buffer you. In my first weeks of sobriety, I was out for dinner with friends, and a complimentary glass of wine appeared in front of me. Without missing a beat, my friend Cheryl, the only one at the table who knew I'd quit drinking, reached over, took the glass and poured it into her own. No one else even noticed.

Bring portable support via your smartphone. There are many online groups for people in recovery, and it is common to see posts from members who are nervous about an event they are attending. Often they will post beforehand to let the group know they may need support throughout the evening. Then they can post a few times for accountability during the event and followup afterward to review how they managed. Popping into the restroom or lobby now and then to check in with online support can make an uncomfortable situation much easier to get through.

If the event is out of town or in an unfamiliar area, consider working in a recovery meeting. If you are a regular attendee of a recovery group, you know how helpful touching base with your program can be on a stressful day. If you have never participated in a meeting before, dropping in as an out-of-town guest can be a little easier than going to one in your own community.

The only meeting I attended in my first two years of recovery was in a large city thousands of miles from home. It was a wonderful experience, and I was able to observe and learn. Later I felt more comfortable seeking out sharing circles, recovery groups, and meetings of various types. You can find meetings in an area with a quick online search, and there are numerous groups to consider including Alcoholics Anonymous, SMART Recovery, Refuge Recovery, Celebrate Recovery, LifeRing, SheRecovers Sharing Circles, and more.

Reflection Exercise:
Stand before a mirror and practice speaking the responses to typical pressure tactics as suggested above. The more you practice saying such phrases, the easier it is to recall them for use in real-time:

- "That's sweet of you to say, but I'm sure you'll all have a great time."
- "I understand. Sorry I can't make it."
- "Have fun. We will get everyone together another time."
- "It doesn't work for me this year, but thank you for the invite."

Tool: Take alongs
As you choose which invitations to accept, prepare the 'take alongs' you will need for each event. A smartphone preloaded with links to message boards, recovery pages, and support groups; a snack and beverage; car keys or cab fare; a thank you gift for the host.

Tips for Friends and Family:

Understand that if your loved one declines an invitation, it's not a rejection of you but a decision to avoid circumstances that may not feel right for them.

Suggest alternatives or adjust plans to include a limited timeframe that better suits them, or release them from the obligation altogether.

The acceptance or decline of invitations may change from year to year as their recovery evolves, so do continue to extend invitations, even if declined in the past.

Do not assume that a person in recovery will not want to attend an event. It may feel considerate to leave them off of the guestlist for an event that will include alcohol, but usually, that is more hurtful than helpful. Leave that decision up to them.

Do consider creating new events or parts of events that are alcohol-free, such as a morning or afternoon meetup.

Focus on ways to spend time together doing activities as an alternative to the usual gatherings focussed solely on food and alcohol.

Wisdom from Sober Friends

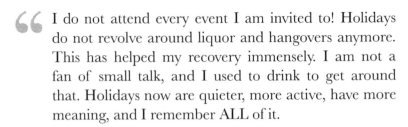

I do not attend every event I am invited to! Holidays do not revolve around liquor and hangovers anymore. This has helped my recovery immensely. I am not a fan of small talk, and I used to drink to get around that. Holidays now are quieter, more active, have more meaning, and I remember ALL of it.

Jan (1 year 10 months of sobriety)

With each invitation I receive, I ask myself why I want to go. I ask myself if I'll be triggered and if I can make a plan wherein I can still enjoy myself.

If not, I bow out gracefully.

Julie (9.5 years of sobriety)

 I definitely am aware of what is going to be happening. I mentally prepare and also allow my self special treats and drinks in the same special fancy glasses as others. Just because we don't partake in the cocktails doesn't mean ours can't feel fancy too.

Lucinda (590 days of sobriety)

FOUR

Family Gatherings

Feeling like a kid again.

Of all the wonders of the holidays, one of the most magical occurrences is the way we can snap right back into our old roles when reunited with our families-of-origin.

I am a fifty-something-year-old grandmother and yet the moment I get together with my mom and sisters, I resume the Baby Sister role: scattered, late, trying to catch up and prove myself. My sense of humour becomes a touch snark-ier, and my feelings are more readily hurt.

I don't like myself that way, and yet the 'little sis' mantle is comfortably around my shoulders before I can even remember to resist slipping into character. I have spent years working to reshape my thinking and behaviour. How can I so readily abandon my restored values?

If you are headed to a family gathering over the holidays and find the prospect stressful, it could be because you are dreading the loss of self that occurs when our old family roles are no longer in alignment with current values. *(Thank you, therapy.)*

Here is what I have learned to do about that:

Choose your part.

By working with a counsellor, I learned that we get through difficult situations by relying on various aspects of our personalities. This becomes dysfunctional when we become dependent on them, and they start to feel like masks we hide behind rather than temporary tools.

For example, by nature, I'm introspective, kindhearted and anxious. During my decades as a business owner, I hid these qualities because I felt they made me weak. I portrayed myself as analytical, tough and confident, and boy did I play the role convincingly. I won awards, gathered accolades, and convinced myself that it was best to keep my weaknesses unknown.

Then, perhaps in a misguided effort to balance out the workload, I started a side project of writing and performing music. I would climb on stage and become a different version, again with fake confidence but also witty and charming in a way meant more to please the crowd than to show my true self.

Not surprisingly, these were the years when I began leaning heavily on alcohol.

Later I told my therapist, "I feel like I created all these fake versions of myself that ended up trapping me and now that I am sober, I need to kill them so I can be authentic."

"Don't kill them," she said. "Use them by choice."

Over the next few sessions, she taught me about Internal Family Systems. I learned that these "fake versions of myself" were just overdeveloped muscles. I had stayed too long in what should have been temporary identities used to get through difficult situations.

The goal going forward became staying grounded in my true self (what I call my Highest Self) and retaining those old abilities to use on occasion - intentionally and as necessary.

So before you walk into that family gathering, decide which version of yourself is the best one for the occasion. You have choices beyond your old family role. The circumstances might call for the Quiet Observer, the Social Butterfly, or the Super Helpful Dish-Doer. Do you need to utilize any of them? Keep your Highest Self in control, make mindful choices, and use the tools at your disposal.

Don't believe everything you think.

Some of the best wisdom comes from recovery meetings and sharing circles. At a SheRecovers retreat on Salt Spring Island, a friend said, "I don't have to buy into every single thing my brain comes up with. Just because I thought it doesn't make it true."

This concept took me by surprise because I hadn't realized I was doing exactly that - letting every thought become a belief.

Byron Katie has some beautiful insights on this process, which she refers to as "The Work." "The Work" begins by asking oneself, "Is that true?"

My family hates me. (Is that true?)

I don't fit in. (Is that true?)

They don't understand me. (Is that true?)

No one ever listens to me in this family! (Is that true?)

Essentially, this inner dialogue is a way of challenging those other parts within. Old emotional wounds can reopen by returning to family-of-origin dynamics, and this may cause your subconscious to brace for impact.

The awakened, wounded part of the mind begins warning that it's necessary to be on guard, that there is danger of becoming hurt.

Watch out, it says, as negative thoughts begin to roll.

It can become a self-fulfilling prophesy, as the raised anxiety causes behaviour to change and creates a heightened response to anything that appears to confirm this bias.

Old patterns aren't always negative.

Many families are harmonious and get along well, yet spending time together still invites old roles and patterns that no longer serve them. It is possible to hold old beliefs that seem positive but have the power to diminish the new patterns a person in recovery is working to embody.

Some examples of this type of thinking can include:

- *I am responsible for holding this family together.*
- *I am the life of the party.*
- *I am the golden child.*

Again, these thoughts can be challenged with the simple question of truth. Although the above statements may seem to involve positive qualities of being strong, fun or good, they are also centred in the perception of others. This can lead to assuming a false role in order to live up to others' expectations, real or imagined.

Lack of conflict does not always equal harmony.

For those fortunate enough to be in a family that gets along nicely and does not experience conflict or drama, togetherness can still cause discomfort. This can be due to the simple disruption of routine that has been created to support recovery or the familiar comfort that makes the other struggles in life seem less important.

Some feelings experienced in this scenario could include:

- *I don't know why I thought I had a problem. I'm fine.*
- *My family is so normal. I have nothing to complain about.*
- *These are people I admire and want to be like. If they can all drink, then I can, too.*

The happiness and solace of old family roles can create a feeling of insulation from everyday life. If there is a part of the subconscious still susceptible to addictive thinking, passivity can become leveraged against sobriety.

I'm fine. I can have a drink. I love these people and want to be like them.

Or there may be no thought given to the urge to drink, and it simply happens as if by rote because the routine and ease of the moment erase all defences.

Another situation that can lead to unexpected wobbliness of sobriety involves families that value peace at any cost. When bad behaviour is ignored for the sake of maintaining peace, there can be undercurrents and hidden feelings of betrayal.

People raised in this type of dynamic may smile and laugh on the outside, but feel hurt and confused on the inside. Often humour is used to mask unkindness, and tolerating it is considered a strength.

When someone stands up for themselves, they may be vilified for pointing out the problem:

- *You take yourself too seriously*
- *Don't be so dramatic*
- *Laugh a little, can't you take a joke?*

Since recovery is a process of untangling the old ways of thinking that don't serve us well, reengaging in the dynamics that led to the development of those patterns can be difficult.

Release yourself from old roles.

No matter whether the old role that seems to take over is positive or negative, just being aware of it can help to make things go smoother.

My therapist explained that these old roles, or parts of self, are tools and can be used mindfully. It is helpful to be able to slip into performer mode or to play the observer or the peacemaker, depending on the situation. The important part is to do so by choice.

When we feel out of control is when we slip into the roles automatically and without thought, only to wonder partway through the evening, *why am I acting this way?*

The better question is, *which role have I slipped into?*

Once you recognize what part of self is surfacing, speak to it.

Thank you for showing up. I know you are trying to help me in this situation, but I've got this. You're welcome to hang out and observe.

So, yes. Talk to yourself. Talk to your parts. Release them from their duties, and put your highest, truest self in charge.

The goal is to live most of your life from this highest, most intentional part of your mind and to only use the extreme 'parts of self' for specific, short-term situations.

Engage through your bubble.

It is possible to remain true to yourself without causing conflict. Gather together the values you hold dear, such as kindness and honesty, and engage through them as a filter for every interaction.

As explained in the earlier chapter on Expectations, imagine a beautiful bubble surrounding you that encases your treasured values. No matter what happens around you, you and your values remain united and protected. Your actions and words are guided by these values, which also have the power to filter incoming messages from others.

Acknowledge true disfunction.

Many feel compelled to attend family events out of loyalty, even though there may be significant dysfunction or problems in the family. If visiting with family involves confrontation with active addiction, abuse, or dramatic conflict, you may decide that it is best to stay away.

If you have attended an event with the best of intentions, only to realize that the situation in which you find yourself is a threat to your sobriety, it is perfectly acceptable to leave. Assuming no one is in danger, you do not need to call out anyone or explain your reason.

Acknowledging family disfunction can be an inside job, an internal reflection on truths which may be denied, ignored, or enabled by other family members. It does not need to be announced or agreed upon by others. Simply accepting the reality of the family and stepping away from the situation can be enough to honour yourself and your sobriety.

When your recovery is disrespected...

Being the only sober person in the family can feel isolating and especially so if your recovery is maligned, intentionally or otherwise. Offhanded comments, a lack of non-alcoholic beverage options, long hours of boozey conversations, games that involve drinking, or story-telling about your previous misadventures can all feel like reminders that you are no longer 'one of them.'

Be patient.

If you are recently sober, it may take a while for your family to comprehend your new lifestyle. Many of us spent years preparing ourselves for the monumental decision to live alcohol-free, struggling to let go of an identity or persona as a social drinker.

Imagine, then, how difficult it must be for our families to change their understanding of us as well. If it takes that long for us to see ourselves in a new way, perhaps it is fair to allow others time to get used to it, too.

Often simple comments can be hurtful because they seem underhandedly critical.

- *It's so typical of you to overcorrect.*
- *If you're an alcoholic, then what does that make the rest of us?*
- *I'm so happy for you that you're finally doing something about your problems!*
- *Oh great, you're going to make the rest of us feel bad.*
- *Yay, you can be the designated driver!*

It is easy to see how statements like these imply that sobriety is unnecessary, or overdue, or inconvenient, or even to be exploited. When people say things like this, they are exposing their own weaknesses, not yours.

Those of us steeped in codependent, people-pleasing thinking can feel derailed by comments that suggest criticism. We often like to control the narrative and feel unsafe when others spin our story.

The wise consensus is to let this go and trust that a new normal will establish itself over time.

Be patient and kind, speak your truth, and don't drink.

Keep some people in your pocket.

One of the very best things about online recovery support is its portability. No matter what is going on around me, I can slip into a quiet corner and post a private message to my group.

Help! I'm at a wedding and the bride and groom are handing out bottles of rum as thank you gifts for the guests. Should I run?

Yes, that actually happened.

The feedback from my online group included tactful ways to navigate the moment…

Say thanks and leave it on a side table for someone else to take away.

…and encouragement for getting through the rest of the event:

Keep your water glass filled and have fun!

There were even shout outs the next day.

You did it! Good for you. Hangover-free mornings never get old!

Being able to post to a support group in real-time is grounding and motivating. Just scrolling through others' updates can be uplifting.

If your family gathering is feeling super sticky and uncomfortable, hide out for a moment and check-in with an online support group, or use the comment section of recovery blogs as a way to reach out. Explain what is happening and ask for feedback, or just let it be known that you are feeling triggered and need reminding of why staying sober is better.

Find a quiet place.

Even when a family gathering is going well, you may feel like hiding under the pile of coats on the spare bed. The bustle, conversations, and tiring activities of the day, combined with the settings, smells, and memories of childhood, can overwhelm.

Being around your family of origin may bring up strong emotions; positive, negative, or mixed. You may find that your ability to regulate such powerful feelings is impaired in the family setting, as nestling into the old birth order and other family dynamics overshadows the coping skills developed for the outside world in adulthood. This can mean feeling unexpectedly weepy or giddy, or in conflict with yourself.

There are many discreet ways to take a break without garnering much attention. Slip outside and walk around the block. The bathroom is a common spot to hide for a few minutes while you massage a bit of lotion onto your feet or the back of your neck. If no one is pounding on the door, do a little stretching while you have some privacy.

If the gathering involves children, drop into their play space to observe or join in. Parents who are obliged to supervise their children will be grateful if you offer to take over for a short stint so they can have some grown-up time. Watching a movie or playing a game with the little ones can be the perfect antidote for mid-party exhaustion.

Many sober friends say they default to kitchen clean-up when the party becomes tiresome. Often the best conversations happen over a sink full of bubbles. The host will appreciate your help, and it can also signal that things are winding down (at least for you!).

Reflection Exercise:

Write a list of any coping roles, masks, or identities you find yourself slipping into in situations with family members. These may relate to your place in the birth (such as the responsible eldest or infantilized youngest) or your role within the family dynamic (jester, scapegoat, or rebel, for example). It's possible to have more than one such role or masks.

Consider the ways that these identities may reflect true aspects of yourself, how they are exaggerations or entirely false, and what purpose they serve.

Next, write what it feels like to be your "Highest Self," referring to times in which you are not wearing a mask or playing a role but intentionally utilizing all of your skills, values, and awareness to the best of your ability.

Finally, recall situations in which each various mask was used, then imagine the same situations with you as your "Highest Self."

Tool: Highest Self Mindset

A conscious effort to draw together all skills, values and awareness in harmony with your deepest, truest, best self. This mindset can be visualized as being encased around you in a bubble to protect and contain these qualities, and through which everything projected is a reflection of the values within. It is from this place that one can ask the question "is that true" as a means to challenge old beliefs and expectations.

Tips for Friends and Family:

Provide a quiet space removed from the crowd that your loved one in recovery can slip off to if they should need a break or time alone. Let them know that this place is available for them, if they wish to use it.

You might even go the extra mile of adding some bottles of water, a few snacks, a blanket, or other comforts.

Just providing this place is an act of support and love, so don't be offended or disappointed if it isn't used.

Have a variety of alcohol-free choices on hand. Be sure they are clearly labelled and openly available. Remember that your loved one may still be discovering what they enjoy, so even if the choices you supply don't appeal to them now, they might be a new favourite in the future.

Especially in early recovery, each outing can be different as new boundaries and coping skills are explored, so be flexible.

Call to follow up after events and discuss possible adjustments for next time.

Respect recovery, it isn't easy.

Meet them where they are at today.

Wisdom from Sober Friends

 [Family gatherings were] always a time to over-drink. I now don't feel that way and let a lot of behaviours that used to trigger me slide. I've detached from other people's issues.

Catherine (20 months of sobriety)

 [Family events are] more uncomfortable than triggering. My parents and sister try not to drink around me, even though I don't mind if they do. This causes them to be sneaky and drink when I'm not there...I swear they pound drinks when I run to the store!

I'd rather they just drink around me because it makes me feel like they are relieved when I exit so they can drink.

Liz (14 months of sobriety)

Initially, [family events were] triggering, and I felt self-conscious and awkward. It has become easier and easier with time. I focus on the food, conversation and chance to be together. I leave events shortly after dessert.

My tolerance or interest in long social events isn't there.

Margaret (5 1/2 years of sobriety)

Being labelled the black sheep, I found that I allowed my family to sabotage my happiness that coincided with me being free from the clutches of alcohol. My narcissistic mother discarded me in 2006, and her flying monkeys, (they are people who act on behalf of the narcissist to a third party, usually for an abusive purpose.) aunts, uncles, cousins, godparents, followed. It was a blessing because my son was only a year old, and I did not want that dynamic transmitted to him. In a toxic family system, it's usually the black sheep who sees through everyone's BS. I had earned a Master's Degree in Social Work and was witnessing my part in this family system. I have worked through the shame and resentment and am continuing to create a family of choice for my son and me.

Barry (427 days of sobriety)

❝ I do [find family events triggering]. I've learned a lot about why I drank! I always felt I had to keep the conversation going, be the life of the party, be louder than I truly am, make everyone comfortable, except ME. I have learned that everyone is in charge of their own experience, their own fun. It is hard for me. I am a natural caregiver. While everyone is drinking their drinks, I have a wonderful non-alcoholic drink on hand. I remember what one drink can do to me, it will become many more. I become someone I am not, and I really don't like that person.

Jan (1 year 10 months of sobriety)

❝ [In my family], we are together all the time, so I have learned to say the serenity prayer. Sometimes out loud! That makes everyone laugh and alleviates tension.

Marci (1064 days of sobriety)

❝ [I'm not triggered by my family of origin], but I do find their drinking annoying. I make sure to have plenty of kombucha, and I let myself indulge in anything I want.

Isabel (2 1/2 years of sobriety)

> I do find it very triggering to attend family gatherings. I have learned I have to put myself and my sobriety first. If I don't feel comfortable, I leave early. When possible, I take friends with me.

Sherri (5 3/4 years of sobriety)

> I no longer find [family events] triggering. I certainly did on Year One, however. I excused myself from company (we are the ones that host most family gatherings) and went to bed early, listening to [recovery] podcasts. My family were most supportive, always saying goodnight and wishing me a good night's sleep...

Marie (900 days of sobriety)

> [Family events] sure can be triggering. I've learned to arrive early and leave early before the drinks flow too much. I make a point to connect with all family members one on one and leave knowing I owe no apologies. I also bring my own beverages.

Julie (9.5 years of sobriety)

> Yes, [family gatherings] can be tough. But I limit my time there and check in with sober friends before, during, and afterwards.

Elizabeth (23 months of sobriety)

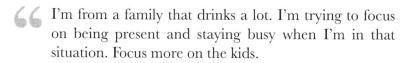

I'm from a family that drinks a lot. I'm trying to focus on being present and staying busy when I'm in that situation. Focus more on the kids.

Jenny (80 days of sobriety)

My first year I was very concerned about Thanksgiving and Christmas. I addressed these by telling my family that I was worried so they would be more mindful of my needs. I also prepared special non-alcoholic beverages and gave myself permission to eat whatever I wanted. I also made sure to take time to myself with some solo walks in the woods.

Amanda (2 years of sobriety)

I pack a travel alter anytime I head to family's houses. Something simple like [essential oils], a few crystals and a journal does the trick. It gives me a special place to escape if I need to. Also, I have learned to not take anything personally. Most of the time people don't mean things the way we receive them. Knowing that helps immensely.

Renee (15 months of sobriety)

FIVE

Hosting an Event

But I'm the host...

It's common for those contemplating sobriety to delay the endeavour until after an upcoming event.

"If I quit now, I won't be able to join the champagne toast at my daughter's wedding."

"There no point in giving up alcohol before the Super Bowl!"

This type of thinking makes the holidays a difficult time to quit.

"I'll quit on January 1st because I have tickets to a gala for New Year's Eve."

"I can't get through spending the holidays with my family without a little rum in the eggnog."

There may never be a convenient window of time on the calendar, and even if there is, it may not necessarily coincide with emotional readiness for making the change, which can come and go.

The fact is that no matter what time of year a person gives up alcohol, eventually the holiday season rolls around. Whether a person has accumulated sobriety counted in months, weeks, days, or hours, the first time encountering the holidays is a new experience.

Erin's Nest

A Bubble Hour guest named Erin told a story about quitting drinking just before Thanksgiving years ago, even though she was scheduled to host a large dinner. She proceeded with the event for family members but took great care to protect her sobriety during the process.

Erin made herself a little nest in her walk-in closet, a comfy pile of pillows and blankets on the floor. She added some snacks, water bottles, and books. Whenever Erin felt overwhelmed during the event, she slipped away from her guests for a "time out" in her special place. She reset her energy, checked in with her online support group, took a sip of water or had a bite to eat, and reemerged ready to continue. No one noticed her absence, as it was just a few minutes here and there.

I love Erin's story because her solution was both simple and radical. She didn't have to go to great lengths to support herself through a difficult challenge, but only had to think outside the usual way of doing things. She also had to permit herself to indulge a little, which can feel uneasy when responsible for the comfort and pleasures of everyone else.

Expectation Assessment

As explained in Chapter 2, it's essential to start with sussing out any unrealized expectations you may have for yourself and others. Some expectations regarding hosting could include:

- how elaborate the decor and menu need to be
- how responsible you are for others having a good time
- what others will contribute
- how grateful people will or will not be
- who gets invited (and who chooses to attend)
- your appearance and behaviour at the event

- if exchanging gifts is expected
- traditions to be honoured

Planning an elaborate decor and menu is fine if you enjoy the extra work involved. The effort becomes burdensome when it's considered a measure of your worth or a reflection of your love. Also, attending to too many unnecessary details may mean neglecting essential self-care like sleeping and eating properly, which can result in cravings for alcohol.

The Surprising Truth About People-Pleasing.

Being a people-pleaser is common among those who struggle with alcohol.

As Melody Beattie explains in "Codependent No More," people-pleasing is a coping skill learned in childhood to get love and attention.

A people-pleaser will disregard their own wishes in order to do what they think others want of them, making a fuss over others in a way that goes above and beyond normal levels of consideration and responsible social interaction.

This behaviour is a form of manipulation, disguised as caring. It is a way to feel safe and in control, and perhaps beyond criticism. Ironically, it is often annoying and anxiety-provoking to others.

If you relate to the description of a people-pleaser, you will find enormous benefit from the work of Beattie and others on the topic of codependency.

For the longest time, I thought the term meant "the spouse of an alcoholic or addict," but it does not. Codependency is the reliance on others for one's definition of self.

On the surface, people-pleasers are excellent hosts. Behind the scenes, however, the extreme efforts to exceed overly high standards can take a toll. A much as they hope to make others happy, it's difficult for them to feel approval even when they get it.

I write this from a place of personal experience. The healing work I have pursued around the subject of codependency and being 'other focussed' has produced some of the most significant and powerful changes in my life.

Something's Gotta Give...

Sobriety can require a little extra planning, so budget time and energy to accommodate your own needs. Avoid the temptation to spend all your resources (time, money, creativity, and enthusiasm) on the event you're hosting, only to find that you've shortchanged your recovery.

Prioritize sobriety because it is the cornerstone of your health and wellbeing.

This may mean that some components of the event are compromised, scaled-back, eliminated, pre-made or hired out. It may mean having gravy from a pouch or store-boughten pie. A simple bouquet of fall leaves could replace the papier-mâché centrepiece your mother-in-law sent you instructions for, and maybe you nap for an hour the day before instead of making hand-calligraphed placecards.

A Few Pointers

- Consider declaring your event alcohol-free. Brunch can have less of an expectation for alcohol to be served than other meals, making it an excellent option.
- If you choose to allow alcohol at your event, ask a friend or family member to be in charge of the bar. Do not expect yourself to handle or serve alcohol. Arrange for help with the cleanup, too. Emptying partially empty glasses can be triggering.
- Have plenty of non-alcoholic options, front and centre. You'd be surprised how many people opt-out of alcohol when given other choices.
- Ask guests to take leftover alcohol home with them. If any booze remains, have a helper dispose of it or take it away.

- If the budget allows, hire out as much of the work as possible. Flowers, food prep, and cleaning services are an excellent investment in your health and wellbeing.

Reflection Exercise:

Imagine the special accommodations you would make for a sober person attending an event at your home. Write out all of the ways you would support a friend in recovery at your party, dinner, or gathering. These are the things you should do for yourself as the host of the event.

Be as kind and thoughtful towards yourself as you are to others.

Tool: A Recovery Nest

Choose a place in your home (or the location of the event to be hosted) that can serve as your own personal getaway. It should have privacy and a comfortable place to sit or lay down and be away from the area where guests will be gathered. Add items that can support short time-outs in this space as a way to reset physically and emotionally: a meditation cushion, headphones and a podcast, snacks, and a bottle of water. Include a timer, which will allow you to relax more deeply without worry that you will fall asleep or stay too long. Even if you don't use this hideaway during your event, just knowing it's available to you can be a comfort.

Tips for Friends and Family:

Do not make assumptions about whether an event hosted by a person in recovery will or will not involve alcohol. The best plan is to discuss this in advance and respect their boundaries and wishes. Some sober hosts have alcohol-free homes, some are comfortable with other people bringing their own alcohol as long as they take it home again afterwards, and some will make full accommodation for guests who wish to drink.

Offer to help with the event by bringing food or helping with preparations. If alcohol is present, offer to look after the serving and clean up of alcoholic drinks. Often the handling of used wine glasses can be just as triggering as pouring drinks, so rinse out glassware and empty bottles. Gather up leftover alcohol and remove it after the event (unless otherwise requested).

Compliment the host on the food and decorations. Show gratitude for their efforts.

Offer to cover the hosting duties for a few minutes here and there to allow them to take a break if needed.

Remember to bring the host a thank you gift that isn't a bottle of wine! Ideas include flowers, a candle, a book, soap or lotion, chocolates, decorative hand towels or dishcloths.

Wisdom from Sober Friends

 I do host during the holidays. I just make sure that I have enough non-alcoholic drinks and to leave the room a lot if people are bothering me.

Catherine (20 months of sobriety)

 I've hosted events, both in my home and have chaired fundraising events at my children's school. I make sure to have at least one sober friend in attendance. I also stock up on my own favourite non-alcoholic drinks and have a 'bring your own booze' policy as well as a 'take it with you when you go' policy.

My only regret looking back is that I probably should have waited longer to play host. I was somewhat uncomfortable the first few times because it was early in my sobriety.

Liz (14 months of sobriety)

" I host Christmas for my family, lots of champagne and wine. For my recovery, I just make sure I have my own drinks.

Laney (3+ years of sobriety)

" [Hosting] is the most difficult kind of event for me because I am a perfectionist and I get quite anxious about how things will 'look' and 'taste'. I use to sip wine while I prepared and definitely after guests left.

I wish I had waited longer to entertain. I know myself better now, and while I like the notion of being a person who likes to entertain, I'm really not. So I do it in stages; one person in for lunch, a couple for dinner.

I don't handle the booze when I entertain. I have other people pour.

Margaret (5 1/2 years of sobriety)

" I do host events again and enjoy them. I don't buy or pour wine but ask those who drink to bring their favourites. Sometimes I explain my sobriety was hard-won, but most people get it and appreciate that I'm not forcing sobriety on them!

I love to create a beautiful display of non-alcoholic

options now. I find that many people prefer having the options.

Diana (25 months of sobriety)

 I let guests know that I have no alcohol and for them to purchase [themselves]. In the past, during sobriety, I would give guests 3x5 index cards with a request to remind me to do something at a specific time. For example: "At 7:00 pm, please remind me to take the rolls out of the oven." "At 8:00, please remind me to start the coffee." In this way, the guests could connect with me, help me so that I did not feel overwhelmed.

Barry (427 days of sobriety)

1. Have my own wonderful beverage in hand and be ready to make more for others who may want to try my beautiful non-alcoholic drink.

2. Never be any two of HALT (Hungry, Angry, Lonely, Tired) at the same time.

3. When it gets to be that time for the party to be over, but there are 'hanger-oners,' say 'It will soon be time to say goodnight.' If they don't get the hint, then add, 'Would you like me to call you a cab?' and get their coats for them.

Kindly dismiss the guests who would otherwise overstay. It could otherwise be far too easy to be taken advantage of as the sober hostess by the over-drinking and unaware guests. Don't let them linger and make asses of themselves. Seriously, it can otherwise go on and on and on, which eventually diminishes the fun of the party. That helps keep it fun for me and shows self-respect. I really love that in my sober life.

Marci (1064 days of sobriety)

" I have [entertained], but everyone present knew I had become alcohol-free, and they were all fully supportive. I made a few mentions of my alcohol-free drink choices at the onset of the night, and it dispelled any awkwardness there may have been.

Kat (157 days of sobriety)

" [I've hosted] a lot of smallish get-togethers. I had all of my favourite non-alcoholic drinks available.

Isabel (2 1/2 years of sobriety)

" I have hosted events in my home since getting sober. Tough stuff! To help support my recovery, I had the event catered so I was not in the kitchen cooking, worrying my head off, and [potentially] drinking. I would recommend that to anyone new in sobriety, or unsure if they could cope. It doesn't have to be catered, maybe potluck, an early afternoon 'bring an appetizer' get together. It takes the pressure off of ME (YOU) to have everyone helping out with the food and in the kitchen.

Jan (1 year 10 months of sobriety)

66 I no longer go over the top! That is huge. When others offer to bring food, I gladly accept and thank them. When drinking, I NEVER accepted help, and it was always way over the top.

Marie (900 days of sobriety)

66 I am very open with others, and generally, nobody drinks very much out of respect.

Julie (9.5 years of sobriety)

66 I've hosted relatively large events, but my family and friends are generally supportive and limit their alcohol use or abstain while at the party.

Elizabeth (23 months of sobriety)

66 I tell them ahead of time that I will not be providing alcohol, but they are welcome to bring some if they'd like. I have young kids, so I allow the day to be focused on them. I have quality conversations with family members I enjoy. I play with my nieces and nephews.

Renee (15 months of sobriety)

66 The stress of "managing everyone's happiness" is always on my mind when we entertain for the holidays (we usually host Thanksgiving, Christmas and sometimes New Year's). In year 2 of sobriety, I had to

finally tell myself over and over (before, during and after) that I was doing ENOUGH - buying and preparing the food, opening up my doors for everyone, and even having the optimal music mix - and if they bring their problems or foul moods, that's their problem, not mine. I still get anxious and worry about all the little details, but I really try to stay relaxed and focused on catching up with people. Before, I would hunker down, drink and numb out, and "busy myself" so I wouldn't really talk with anyone. I've made an effort to change that.

Michellene (2 1/2 years of sobriety)

SIX

Replacement vs. Transfer

Trade this for that

After becoming alcohol-free, it takes a while to find replacements. I'm not just talking about what's in your glass, although that's important.

The habit of consuming alcohol as a go-to for emotional and social comfort must be substituted with alternatives that do double-duty by consoling alcohol cravings on top of the initial problem that triggered it in the first place.

The process of addiction causes interest in other pastimes and comforts to wane until the addictive substance is the only solace. Alcohol becomes the first thing that springs to mind the moment any emotion is experienced, good or bad. This is learned behaviour over time, and new ways of coping can only emerge if pursued.

New coping skills that emerge are called *replacement behaviours*.

Dopamine downregulation

What's tricky about finding suitable replacement behaviours is that people who are affected by addiction are also caught in an exaggerated dopamine response cycle. You know the good feeling that would wash over you as you reached for a drink, that relief when the craving was strong, and a drink was in sight? The first moments of joy as you sipped? That wasn't the alcohol; it was dopamine.

Dopamine is a chemical released in the brain and is responsible for pleasurable feelings. When a dopamine release occurs repeatedly, it not only causes a pleasure response but also starts to set up reward-seeking behaviour.

We all remember the example of Pavlov's dogs, an experiment in which animals were observed to salivate when a bell rang to signal feeding time. The dog's developed a conditioned response to the mere *anticipation* of food.

I've received thousands of emails from people who feel trapped by their addiction to alcohol. They often express the same confusion that I once felt as well:

I don't know what's wrong with me. I'm a strong person, but I can't help myself when it comes to alcohol.

There is nothing *wrong* with a person who becomes addicted to an addictive substance. That is the normal response. We easily understand that this is true for cigarettes and hard drugs, but for some reason, we're perplexed by the addictive powers of alcohol.

That helpless feeling around alcohol (and other habit-forming substances) is due in part to the conditioned dopamine response. Getting to the drink causes an initial flood of good feelings. Then alcohol goes to work as a depressant, causing other brain chemicals to alter and lessen the feel-good emotions. The result is a spike of fleeting positive feelings followed by a dampening of emotions.

The clever brain adapts to the elevated levels of dopamine by tolerating higher and higher levels before responding with the associated positive feelings, a process known as downregulation, which elevates the reward-seeking behaviour. But then the alcohol also suppresses emotions, good and bad.

What a treacherous cycle!

The pleasure-reward circuitry of the brain is thrown out of balance, but it persists and, like a washing machine on spinning an uneven load, this ability to keep going causes things to go sideways.

Harnessing the power of dopamine

The good news is that this pleasure-reward cycle can be leveraged to support sobriety.

Other things can also cause a natural release of dopamine. These include touch sensations like having a massage or petting dog, listening to music, exercise, meditation, getting lots of sleep and eating a balanced diet.

It is vital to explore new ways of doing things day-to-day that can produce pleasurable feelings. Develop an arsenal of comforts that you can turn to instead of alcohol.

Remember that this is a conditioned response and takes some time to evolve. Repeat positive activities daily, and soon you'll find that you not only look forward to them but that they give you satisfaction. Furthermore, good feelings persist longer without alcohol's depressive effects.

Without discovering and reinforcing new patterns of pleasure and comfort, it can be tough to self-soothe in a triggering situation. Whether it's the presence of alcohol that causes a craving or a strong emotional response (positive or negative) that calls for numbing, the replacement behaviour will be less effective if it has not been in place for a while.

If you haven't done so already, get busy with the assignment of discovering and reinforcing new forms of comfort and pleasure!

Transfer of addictive behaviours

Of course, there's a catch.

It seems that individuals who have experienced addiction are also more susceptible to becoming hooked on certain comforting behaviours known as *process addictions*.

Process addictions are pleasure-inducing behaviours that become obsessive and habitual, despite the absence of an addictive substance. These behaviours can include gambling, sex, pornography, eating, shopping, exercising, computer games or internet use.

Although anyone can develop a process addiction, the overlap with substance addictions is likely due to similar underlying issues that include genetics, a history of trauma, social influences and stress.

There's no way to avoid most sources of process addiction; they're part of everyday life. We have to eat to survive, and we have to shop to eat. The same internet usage and social media that can become problematic are a significant source of recovery-related support and information. Sex is an inherent part of our humanity. Exercising is good for us.

Many people report getting through the early days of sobriety by crawling under a blanket with a pizza and a bag of gummy bears, using video games and television to pass the time.

That's okay, just don't drink.

Even if the new routines and behaviours aren't ideal, they can be tweaked later. The first order of business is to break up with booze.

Sometimes old problems reemerge after a person quits drinking, like the resurgence of a latent eating behaviour or overspending habit. The term *whack-a-mole* is often used to describe this phenomenon, referring to a carnival game in which the player attempts to bop mechanical rodents popping randomly from multiple holes. It's a fitting picture of how it feels to conquer one problem and discover another.

The process of healing that goes beyond sobriety into recovery addresses the underlying issues of both substance and process addictions. Therefore therapy, treatment, working a recovery program, and/or pursuing self-directed forms of treatment can bring lasting change.

Our purpose here is to find ways to get through holiday-related situations, so the main point is to understand what process addictions are and why you may be susceptible to them.

The holidays and transfer behaviours

Having established that replacement behaviours are beneficial and that some replacement behaviours have the potential to become process addictions, it is important to understand how certain aspects related to the holiday season can become problematic.

Shopping and spending

As the holidays are a time of gift-giving, shopping and spending can quickly get out of hand. This may be further compounded for those who are codependent or people-pleasers, as discussed in Chapter 3, because feelings of self-worth and validation are dependent on making other people happy. Going overboard on gift-giving is a common symptom of this mindset.

If financial pressures result from overspending on gifts, the stress of paying the bills will quickly counter pleasure derived from giving. For those with greater means, giving excessively can still fail to produce lasting pleasure if it isn't met with the expected amount of appreciation or because the same levels of generosity may not be reciprocated, leading to resentment (as discussed in Chapter 2).

Talk to the people with whom you exchange gifts and agree on a budget, which can help establish boundaries around spending and head off any unrealized expectations related to gift-giving.

Making simple gifts can also be an excellent alternative. Creative activities spark dopamine production and can be more budget-friendly (beware - many crafting enthusiasts can attest to the potential to overspend on supplies and gadgets!). Again, it's important to avoid grandiosity and expectations, so keep the emphasis on gifts that are simple and thoughtful.

Overindulging in food

Not only do many celebrations seem to revolve around eating during the holidays, but also the foods on offer tend to be extravagant. The delectable appetizers, roasted meats with festive sauces and side dishes, iced cookies and desserts so rich that they're reserved for special occasions. Then there are the gifts of food that roll in, only to sit on the counter as a source of temptation: foil-wrapped chocolates, candied nuts, spiced pretzel mix, and caramel popcorn in decorative tins.

The generally accepted wisdom is that if eating helps you abstain from alcohol, then it is better to overeat temporarily than to relapse and drink (this, of course, assumes that you are not in treatment for a co-occurring eating disorder, in which case you should have a plan in place to deal with multiple triggers).

Food can be a successful behaviour replacement for alcohol because of the pleasure derived from eating.

As Chris Engen of Nutrition for Recovery related on a recent Bubble Hour episode, managing blood sugar levels can make an even bigger difference in the effectiveness of food as a drinking deterrent.

"Many alcoholics mistake a blood sugar crash for alcohol cravings," says Engen. "It's important to eat protein every 3-4 hours, especially in high-risk situations. Hunger is the number one trigger for relapse. Be sure you're not starving when you get there! Getting too hungry and the subsequent blood sugar crash will cause your brain to go offline, and may have you reaching for alcohol before you can access the prefrontal cortex of your brain, where good decisions and choices are made."

While eating something sweet might give a helpful boost of dopamine to combat feelings of discomfort that can trigger alcohol cravings, sugary foods eaten on their own can set off a spike and crash cycle of blood sugars. To balance this out, Engen recommends that sweets should always be consumed with servings of fibre, fat, and protein to help level out the effect on the bloodstream.

So when filling your plate, be sure to include the protein offerings, such as meats, cheese, nuts, and a few veggies, in addition to the treats. This will help you manage any alcohol cravings and also leave you feeling more satiated and balanced for a longer period of time.

When does a replacement behaviour become an addiction transfer?

Replacement behaviours are better choices that not only soothe the need for comfort but may also have positive benefits. A glass of sparkling water with lemon is not only alcohol-free, but it is hydrating.

Staying sober creates space for healing, as we have more time, awareness and emotional capacity to devote to recovery endeavours. Reading self-help books, going to sharing circles, spending time in therapy or journaling, are all ways of filling the hours that used to be spent numbing out with intoxication.

Newcomers to Alcoholics Anonymous are often encouraged to attend daily meetings for the first three months of sobriety, which is a means of developing a replacement behaviour while simultaneously building relationships with others in recovery and absorbing the information through the personal stories shared in meetings.

It is perfectly fine to use potential sources of addiction transfer as a distraction or pastime to support recovery, provided that the activities are not taking over one's life and causing adverse side effects. If the behaviour becomes isolating or causes neglect of regular responsibilities or other negative consequences, then it should raise concerns.

Many people find there is a particular span of each day that is most difficult, a time often referred to as 'the witching hour.' This is most often late afternoons and/or evenings when the busy-ness of the day gives way to a need to unwind or decompress. (If a cycle of daily physical addiction is underway, this period will coincide with the effects of the previous day's alcohol intake wearing off, and therefore may well be a matter of withdrawal symptoms causing the craving for more alcohol.)

It can be a crucial time to stay occupied and comforted, so activities that are pleasantly distracting are ideal. A large mug of tea or glass of bubbly water and a mindless video game can help pass the hours until bedtime. However, if it seems impossible to stop the game and go to bed, resulting in a neglect of the basic need for sleep, then the behaviour is ultimately detrimental.

Sometimes it is hard to see the correlation. In her memoir "My Fair Junkie," author Amy Dresner chronicles a harrowing descent into sex addiction when she got sober from drugs and alcohol. However, she was unable to see the connection between these two aspects of her life. Amy began to isolate from friends and take dangerous risks for the sake of feeding her compulsion to meet strangers for sex, which she told herself was empowering and fulfilling. It wasn't until she began to address some of the underlying issues contributing to both the original and transfer addictions that she was able to feel in control and to ultimately let go of a pattern that had taken over her life with many negative consequences.

It is important to be aware of the behaviours that have the potential to become process addictions and to engage in them with caution. Though they can be effective short-term tools to pass the time or negate cravings, they also have the potential to take away from the whole-hearted life of freedom that you are pursuing as a person in recovery.

Reflection Exercise:
Think about the activities you enjoy that have the potential to become process addictions. Consider some guidelines for yourself to help keep these activities in check. For example, make a budget for unnecessary shopping, use the settings on electronic devices to monitor and limit the amount of time spent on games or social media, and write out any red flags you can be watchful for regarding potentially problematic pastimes. Be especially mindful that the holiday season emphasizes extra spending and eating.

Tool: Replacement Behaviours
Healthy alternatives to an addictive behaviour or substance that help to bring comfort while supporting recovery.

Tips for Friends and Family:
Keep an eye out for warning signs of addiction transfer, such as prolonged isolation and avoidance of regular responsibilities in favour of an activity with process addiction potential. While accusations or advice are not helpful, do voice observations neutrally and ask questions to help spark awareness. Communicate simply:

"I notice you're doing a lot of (activity). How is that going for you?"

Since change begins with awareness (see *Stages of Change* in Chapter 10: Terms), raising your concerns can incite the process of change.

Remember that activities with the potential to become process addictions can also be effective short-term substitutions for the original addiction. Encourage and support your loved one as they pursue recovery-related activities (meetings or groups, therapy, consuming recovery materials, working with a coach, physical activity and self-care) that will contribute to their overall understanding and healing of the issues underlying the addiction. As this work progresses, other symptoms like process addictions can slowly resolve.

Wisdom from Sober Friends

66 I've had some trouble with binging. Instead of eating a couple of squares of chocolate, I sometimes eat a whole bar. And in the beginning, I'd drink so much LaCroix that I'd get a stomach ache. I try to focus on the task at hand - not drinking alcohol. And, when I start eating my third bowl of cereal, I sometimes just halt the behaviour and throw it out. I do find (as cliched as it sounds) to be mindful of what I'm putting in my mouth and just thinking about it - I can usually manage my behaviour. And you know what, if I feel like I want to eat a whole bag of popcorn, I do it. I follow a very healthful diet, work out every day, and take care of myself -- and I love popcorn, so why not?

Michellene (2 1/2 years of sobriety)

66 [I filled the void with] eating, playing tennis, going to graduate school. Overeating to numb out [became problematic]. [Balance] starts with awareness, moves to accountability. I can get into over-functioning and perfectionism. [I've learned to] let go and set healthy intentions.

Kathy (31 years of sobriety)

"" I'm trying to work on intuitive eating as the food issues are primary. The balance is really hard because eating sugar is much better than drinking, but I don't like feeling out of control with anything. It makes me feel bad about myself. A coping skill should make you feel healthier and proud of managing stress in a positive light. I'm not against sugar, [just] continuing to eat mindlessly or even continuing to eat after telling myself I should stop.

Holly (2 years of sobriety)

"" I coped by running and eating sweets. I still struggle with eating sweets. I can get addicted to anything, good or bad. It can be fitness, eating, shopping. Awareness is the key to recognizing self-destructive behaviours. I'm in 12-step recovery and have a sponsor I meet with regularly. The holidays and other things are no longer a trigger for me.

Lelani (3 1/2 years of sobriety)

"" Initially, I started smoking cigarettes a lot more, which was bad. Over time I had to learn to take way better care of myself. A helpful thought was to remember that when I crave alcohol or another way to numb, what I am really looking for is comfort. With that in mind, I try to pay attention to what I really need in the moment and what would make me feel better. Often it's cooking, listening to a podcast, connecting with close friends, or just going to bed early with a good book.

Marine (16 months of sobriety)

Positive [new behaviours]: exercise, meditation, new hobbies like jigsaw puzzles. Negative [new behaviours]: spending a lot of time playing games on my phone, eating sugar. I think the amount of time I spend on my phone is the most problematic behaviour I currently have. It takes me away from the things that really matter. I know it's a coping skill when I don't feel worse after doing it. I have to tune into my emotions for the first time in my life. I never feel awful after taking a bath or going on a walk. But I do feel worse when I eat a ton of gummy bears or play 47 rounds of a game on my phone. One is a coping skill. The other is decidedly not.

Sarah (500 days of sobriety)

SEVEN

Work Obligations

Work Mode

Almost everyone finds it necessary to separate private and public identities to some degree. When it comes to our professional lives, this separation may feel distinct and defined or somewhat overlapped.

Given the vast array of work scenarios and individual human experience, it's necessary to make some broad assumptions for this discussion. Let's agree that, generally speaking, some common factors of most work environments include:

- a requirement for some degree of professional decorum
- that coworkers have limited exposure to one another's lives outside of work
- that clients have limited knowledge of one's life outside work
- that the expectation for professionalism extends to work-related social gatherings
- that some type of year-end or holiday event is typical

Adaptation to Work Environment

Professional decorum sounds lofty, but it's part of every job. A grocery clerk is required to be efficient and courteous. An accountant needs to be informed and discreet. A salesperson should be personable and motivated.

Beyond the demands of performance, there is often also a need to conform to an organization's work culture, which can range from intense and serious to lighthearted and playful.

Between decorum and culture, the work environment may require assuming behaviours and attitudes that are not entirely natural. These accommodations must be within a person's capacity, or else it would be impossible to continue the work effectively for any length of time.

Drawing forward certain aspects of our personalities to fit a situation is sometimes referred to as the "adaptive state."

The adaptive state differs from the extreme roles and masks discussed in Chapter 4 because it does not involve betraying personal values or going to extremes.

For example, a quiet-natured person whose job requires a certain level of communication will adapt by talking as much as is necessary, more than they naturally prefer. Others may have to make an effort to be less chatty at work to meet the standard of interaction expected. Both are adaptations, but neither go against a personal value.

There is often a feeling of "shifting gears" after work, as we transition from our adaptive, professional mode to our natural state in private life.

Recovery and Workplace Vulnerability

Considering that work involves a constant shifting back and forth between the natural and adaptive state, it's no wonder that making a significant life change like sobriety can feel strange in the workplace.

Sobriety can feel like a monumental shift that changes how we see everything, which can mean that both the adaptive and natural state shift too. If a person is feeling more vulnerable and raw in their private life, gearing up to put on the "game face" for work can seem extra daunting.

Additionally, many people feel that their professional identity is jeopardized by anyone knowing that they are in recovery because they fear judgement for having experienced alcohol dependency. I've received emails from teachers, doctors, babysitters, therapists and others who worried that their clients would lose confidence in them if their sobriety was revealed. Elected officials have a fear of scandal that is certainly understandable in the current climate of privacy violations and public humiliations.

Conversely, I've also heard from salespeople who are expected to "wine and dine" clients and go along with whatever level of recreational celebration the corporate culture demands of them in order to close a deal. They feel that their success in sales is seriously hindered by the inability to continue participating in the complimentary indulgences for clients, even though those activities may well have contributed to a problematic alcohol relationship.

Attitudes towards recovery are changing fast in this information age, and many are realizing that sobriety is a strength. The fear of discovery is understandable but not always realistic, especially in early recovery when one's self-perception can be skewed.

Personally, I initially believed that sobriety meant I was weak and broken. I'd worked hard to sustain an image of strength and untouchability in my career, so work was not a place I wanted to be open and vulnerable.

The feeling of *imposter syndrome* (see Terms in Chapter 10) that contributed to alcohol use in the first place worsened for a while. This changed over time, as I did some work on core beliefs.

Once I got stronger within myself, I felt less of a need for the people around me to have an exaggerated impression of me. I was able to be more real and comfortable in all aspects of my life.

Work-related Social Events

Work-related social events are sticky to begin with. Daily interactions in the workplace involve finding the balance between the natural and adaptive state, plus assessing the decorum required for the job and playing to the work culture. Social events related to work include showing a bit of your personal side, but not so much as to undermine your professionalism come Monday morning.

It's as if the annual Christmas party or year-end gala are an in-between zone, giving coworkers and possibly clients a glimpse at who you are away from the day-to-day workplace. Your clothing choices, accompanying guest, and social behaviours are show another side of you.

Often this is a great thing. Learning more about each other deepens relationships and strengthens bonds between coworkers. But it can also go sideways, and we've likely all seen it at some point. Some have lived it. Some have the photocopy of their own bum to prove it....

The Professional/Social Grey Zone

For a person in recovery, this grey zone between the public and private self has some additional complications. Some may want to keep their sobriety entirely under wraps, trying to navigate a drinking environment without letting on that they are abstaining. Others may have past experiences to reconcile, such as leading the drinking culture at work, and in sobriety must reestablish a different identity. Most of us are somewhere in between.

If you feel uneasy about work-related occasions, this can explain why. The changes undertaken in recovery involve new understanding, rethinking our core beliefs. It can be easy to separate this deep, personal reflection from the adaptive state in which we go to our jobs.

We generally save recovery for our natural state of mind when we are in a safe, private environment. To borrow an image from Brene Brown, this is "bento box" thinking, wherein parts of life are cleaned up and compartmentalized. There is no grey zone in a bento box, and you must find your own way to bridge the parts.

For those of you who were formerly known as the "life of the party" and worry that you'll be seen as dull and boring without alcohol, take heart. Some people may have loved your old antics, but surely some were at the very least indifferent. Either way, there are other ways to connect with others.

Instead of trying to live up to the things you used to *do*, think about the way you made others *feel*. For example, if drinking helped you to be more boisterous and funny, those around you likely felt carefree. If you had a bottle in each hand as you led a conga line, those who fell in behind you felt engaged. If sober you isn't likely to be as boisterous or outgoing, it's still possible to make others feel carefree and engaged another ways.

Consider the Purpose.

When preparing to attend work-related social functions, first consider the purpose of the event. This is two-fold. Why is the event being held in the first place, and what is *your* purpose in attending? Consider your obligations from both perspectives and create some tangible outcomes.

- Is the event mandatory? To what extent are you required to be involved?
- Are there expected results to be achieved, such as raising funds, closing a sale, accepting an award, or being photographed and seen?
- Are there parts of the event that appeal to you and parts that do not?

Even if you're comfortable attending, it is still worth your while to reflect on the purpose and goals related to the event. It will help to add some clarity and deliverables, lessening the possibility of triggers in the social "grey zone."

Having a mental "to do" list for the evening can make it easier to leave when the time comes, knowing the boxes are all checked. It is only then a matter of your own comfort and enjoyment guiding the decision to stay or go.

The "Plus One"

Most of these events are designed to include a "plus one." Whomever you bring along should be supportive of your recovery and informed of your goals for the evening.

This may be a new concept for couples who have socialized in the same way for years and have old patterns and routines when it comes to attending events together. It can also feel awkward if you are not in a relationship and invite a date that you don't know very well.

It may be necessary to rethink your choice of companion altogether.

Bringing a guest who plans to enjoy the open bar and dance until dawn may no longer be sympatico with your alcohol-free lifestyle. There should be a mutual understanding and agreement of what your level of comfort is with your companion's drinking, and also with their willingness to help you stay alcohol-free.

When my husband and I were learning to navigate social situations in my early sobriety, he was great about going directly to the bar to order alcohol-free drinks for me. He even took care to watch as they were prepared to be sure that I wasn't served alcohol by mistake. If someone handed me a drink unexpectedly, my husband discreetly set it aside.

At one event, he even tipped a bartender to run across the street and buy my beverage of choice since it wasn't available onsite. Another time he smuggled my alcohol-free drinks into a restaurant in his coat pockets. We always agreed that I could take the car home whenever I felt ready and, if he wanted to stay, he would take a cab later.

As I got more adept at handling various social situations, there were also times when I chose to attend alone or take a friend, depending on the purpose and goals I'd determined for the event.

Chapter 2 explored the dangers of expectations and resentments. Agreeing on a plan ahead of time can help to eliminate mismatched expectations and, subsequently, avoid hard feelings afterward.

Do Have Fun!

It is important to note that having fun is possible, even likely. It can be very freeing to be sober under these circumstances because the obsession of managing our drinking in front of others is no longer a burden.

When I was drinking problematically, it was rarely in front of others. I sipped wine at home before an event to quell social anxiety and then afterward to ease the tension of trying to minimize and control my alcohol use in public. I'd spend the whole evening waiting to go home and drink privately. Being alcohol-free is a cakewalk compared to my old ways!

Whether your relationship with alcohol was secret or public, you'll notice a big difference without it.

Conversations are more sincere and memorable. Dancing is lighthearted and fun. Food is it's own enjoyment and merely watching the others in the room can be fascinating.

Another benefit is that social blunders, like forgetting someone's name or mispronouncing a word, doesn't carry the weight of shame that we may have given to drunken mistakes. We can apologize and move on without beating ourselves up on a million different levels.

Go, have a great time, tick of the to-do boxes and leave when you're ready.

Well done!

Reflection Exercise:

Make a list of goals to achieve at work-related functions: networking, volunteer requirements, bid on the silent auction, hear the guest speaker, say hello to coworkers' family members, etc.

Make an effort to accomplish this list of goals within the first hour of the event and then give yourself permission to leave the moment you decide it is time, knowing that you have done your duty by attending.

If you are comfortable and are enjoying yourself, then you can stay as long as you like!

Tool: Delayed Gratification

Have a planned reward to look forward to immediately after the event: a lovely bath, a new book, a sweet treat. Celebrate your successful navigation of the evening by coming home to a pre-planned treat.

Tips for Friends and Family:

If you are accompanying a sober friend or family member to a work event, be sure to keep an eye on their glass and help them keep it filled with a safe beverage of their choosing.

Be supportive without making a show of it to others.

Either plan to leave whenever they are ready or arrange to have separate transportation if it is likely that you may want to stay longer.

Discuss this in advance and agree on options so that the evening can unfold smoothly.

Wisdom from Sober Friends

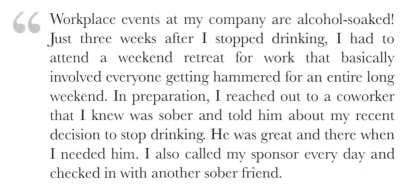 Workplace events at my company are alcohol-soaked! Just three weeks after I stopped drinking, I had to attend a weekend retreat for work that basically involved everyone getting hammered for an entire long weekend. In preparation, I reached out to a coworker that I knew was sober and told him about my recent decision to stop drinking. He was great and there when I needed him. I also called my sponsor every day and checked in with another sober friend.

The craziest part was the realization after the weekend was over that I actually had a good time without alcohol. That was a huge turning point for me. I also felt fine every morning when all of my coworkers were hungover and sick, so that was a definite positive of being sober.

Liz (14 months of sobriety)

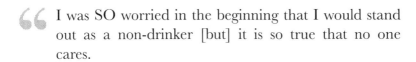 I was SO worried in the beginning that I would stand out as a non-drinker [but] it is so true that no one cares.

Laney (3+ years of sobriety)

I do attend professional events that involve alcohol, and it does not bother me at all. I go with friends that know I am in recovery. We leave early before it gets crazy.

Sherri (5 3/4 years of sobriety)

> I removed myself from the circle I was involved with before, all of whom are heavy, consistent drinkers. At professional events, I have been at ease saying no thank you when offered alcohol, but always take someone with me who knows my struggle and can provide support in a moment of weakness.

Kat (157 days of sobriety)

> I am very proud of my sobriety. I do not mind if people notice that I don't drink. I always have a nonalcoholic beverage in hand, so nobody asks if they can get me a drink! I leave when I see the alcohol starting to hit people, or before. While I am there, I make contact with as many people as I can. I try and find out one thing new about a person that I don't know a lot about.

Jan (1 year 10 months of sobriety)

> I check in with sober friends before, during, and afterwards. Self-care beforehand (meditation, yoga, journaling, baths). A treat (dessert, a bubble bath, popcorn) to look forward to afterwards. Checking in with sober friends is huge. It's like a touchstone to keep me on track.

Elizabeth (23 months of sobriety)

EIGHT

Socializing

It Gets Easier.

Many people in recovery identify their alcohol use as a coping tool for social anxiety. Others find that they had settled into an identity as "the life of the party" and felt obligated to be having fun in a showy way. Although the two reasons for drinking may seem like opposites, they both have a root in wanting to please others.

Once a person quits drinking, they are considered to be sober. When they being to explore the reasons behind their excessive drinking and address those issues, recovery has begun.

The further a person gets into the realm of changed behaviours in recovery, the easier socializing often becomes.

Previous chapters have touched on the expectations we place on ourselves and others, as well as people-pleasing or codependency, and the pitfalls of slipping into old family roles or transferring to other maladaptive behaviours. Armed with this information, you may find that social situations become easier.

We've reviewed some of the challenges around family events, being a host, and attending work-related functions.

What about plain old socializing?

Spending time with friends is obviously less complicated than the intricacies of family dynamics and professional obligations. However, there can be circumstances that make socializing difficult, including:

- Friendships that used to revolve around drinking
- Any damaging interactions you may have had when drinking
- Being excluded from invitations because of your sobriety
- Being invited but not accommodated as a sober guest
- Feeling unsure of yourself around alcohol
- Having a partner who wants to socialize differently than you
- Social anxiety that was previously self-medicated with alcohol

Shifting Friendships

It can be a painful realization that past alcohol use resulted in the curation of friendships to support our patterns. Many of the people who we thought were good friends may have simply been companion drinkers and enablers. This is hard to accept because it not only means the other person wasn't a true friend but also that we weren't acting sincerely either. Or perhaps those relationships were built with good intentions, but have run their course.

This happens.

Before discarding these friendships entirely, I suggest testing their ability to shift.

Create new ways of socializing that don't include alcohol. Invite your old drinking buddies to your favourite coffee shop on a Sunday morning and ask about their work, hobbies, and families. Ask what they've binge-watched on tv lately, or if they can recommend their favourite author.

Ask yourself:

- *Do I like these people?*
- *Do I enjoy their company?*
- *Do I trust and respect them?*

If the answer is yes, then you will probably find that your ability to socialize together can adapt to your new circumstances. However, if it becomes evident that your relationship is doesn't have the potential to grow, it may be time to rethink your social circles.

The phrase "release with gratitude" is a positive way to frame letting go of a friend. There is no need for confrontation or formality, simply accept that you need to move on to new relationships. You never know when these old friends may make changes of their own that cause them to reenter your life again under other circumstances.

Meanwhile, a different reversal can also happen.

Friends that you may have lost interest in, due to your old drinking habits, can be rediscovered in recovery. Those neighbours you stopped inviting over because they'd only drink tea and go home early, or the ones that go hiking bright and early on Saturday mornings, or the people who made you feel awkward because they'd nurse a drink for hours while you kept filling your glass. Without alcohol as a barrier, there may be commonalities to rediscover.

If your recovery includes a program or group, you will also have some new friends, as well. These are sometimes arm-length support people, but often deep connections develop. Many recovery groups plan special events for members or have regular meetups and other outings.

Consider the relationships you give your energy to and allow them to change as necessary.

Baggage and history

Hey, remember that New Year's Eve party when you…

You may be socializing with people who have witnessed past behaviour that feels shameful. You may have offended others or hurt them in the past, embarrassed yourself, or have unresolved issues. You may have been given a pass because you acted while intoxicated, or your actions may be an uncomfortable secret you keep. You may not even remember what happened, but know something went down.

The twelve-step recovery process involves confronting these issues head-on in a formal action known as *making amends*.

An amend is more than a simple apology. It means speaking with the person you've harmed to take responsibility for the hurt you've caused and taking steps to repair the damage.

Bob, I'm the one who threw up on your rug at least years party. I pretended it wasn't me and left it for you to find the next day. I know you've already dealt with it, but here is a gift certificate for a cleaning service. I'm sorry, and I promise to be more honest in the future.

Marci, I yelled at you that time you took my keys away and refused to let me drive after I'd been drinking. I called you names and told other people an untrue version of the story for a long time afterward. I am sorry. You may have saved my life that night. I am grateful for your actions, and I have told the truth about that incident to everyone who heard my false account.

If it's impossible to fix the damage or if confronting the person would harm them, the process can be done indirectly as well. The important thing is to take responsibility for the issue and take corrective action.

Whether you are involved in a twelve-step program or not, the concept of making amends is powerful in healing relationships. It can ease tensions that may exist in your circle of friends as you move forward under the new circumstances of your sobriety.

Feeling Left Out

Many have described seeing photos of a party on social media and realizing that they weren't invited to a gathering, presumably because of their sobriety. It can be incredibly painful and leaves a sober person feeling confused and betrayed.

There are two likely reasons this happens.

The group of friends may well fall into the category of "drinking buddies" and is no longer a great fit, as described above.

The other reason could be that the friend group is considerate but misguided, and wrongly thought that it was a kindness to avoid putting a sober friend in a drinking situation.

If you should have this experience or wish to avoid it, the solution is simple. First, be sure that these are friendships you want to maintain. If they are, an honest conversation is in order.

Let them know that you appreciate their attempt to be considerate of your sobriety but talk about other ways that it can be managed without excluding you. They might be surprised to learn that it would be more empowering for you to be invited and have the choice of whether or not to attend.

They might also be interested to learn some of the ways you manage social gatherings, like bringing your own drinks and having an option to leave early.

Some of the best advice I received in early sobriety was from my friend, Dixie, who had a family member in recovery and knew tons of tips.

If you always show up with a few cans of your favourite soda, before you know it, your friends will make sure they keep some on hand for you.

She was so right! Not only that, but within a few months, my friends would text me from the grocery store before a party with pictures of different kinds of bubble water and mocktails they were discovering.

Look, I got a variety of things for you to try tonight!

My friend Cheryl is a thoughtful host who not only keeps an array of non-alcoholic drinks for me but also puts out little dishes of fruit to mix into them. She makes sure I have a pretty glass, too.

Not everyone will be so considerate, so you will have to be your own best friend at times.

Bring your beverage of choice wherever you go. Keep a cooler of it in your car, just in case. Often the only non-alcoholic choices are the kids' drinks, so unless you bring your own you may find yourself sucking on a lukewarm juice box.

Hanging with the Normies

Some people rigidly protect their sobriety by avoiding any and all situations that include alcohol. Many go to the other extreme, navigating sobriety in a sea of booze. Most settle for something in between.

The added commitments around the holiday season will bring many opportunities to test and refine your position.

My personal belief is that I need to function in a world that includes alcohol. I permit occasional social drinking in my home but don't personally handle or serve alcohol.

Away from home, I will eat food items that contain cooked alcohol in the recipe, such as pasta sauces, and avoid foods drizzled with liquors, like Tiramisu. We do not cook with wine at home.

Our circle of friends are "normies," or normal drinkers, by which I mean they drink socially without becoming overtly intoxicated, so going out for dinner or to a party with friends usually means there will be alcohol on the table.

I'm comfortable around others who are drinking, but not around anyone who is drunk. When drinkers begin slurring or acting silly, I call it a night. If the main event is something that can't accommodate participating alcohol-free, like a scotch tasting or a wine pairing dinner, I either decline the invite altogether or make a short appearance early in the evening.

These are my choices, my boundaries. It took me some trial and error to develop them, but in time I learned what served my recovery.

It's important to create guidelines to help you navigate social situations. Abstinence-based sobriety is non-negotiable: *we don't drink no matter what.* How you manage that is up to you.

Having rules allows something other than your feelings to guide you because emotions aren't always logical or trustworthy. You may be used to ignoring your inner voice, especially if you are a people-pleaser, so your principles allow you to stay objective and firm.

Social Mismatches

It is essential to have an ongoing open dialogue about your boundaries regarding social situations with your partner or support person. If you are attending events together, they must be aware of your personal rules and supportive of your sobriety. It is also necessary to listen to their perspectives and accept how they prefer to enjoy their social time. If there is a mismatch, this must be discussed and negotiated.

Some partners give up alcohol as a show of support, but many do not. If your goal is to avoid drunkenness at an event, but your partner's goal is to let loose by indulging fully, or some other mutually exclusive scenario, you need a plan you can agree on. Perhaps one of you goes, and the other does not. Maybe you leave early, and your partner stays late. Possibly one of you sleeps in the guest room, not as a punishment but as an agreed-upon strategy.

What you decide together is up to you, but it must be talked about ahead of time.

Do not make assumptions or take it as it comes. Talk it over in advance and then follow up afterward to make adjustments for next time.

Social Anxiety

I've lost count of the number of guests on The Bubble Hour podcast who say that they started drinking in their teens to deal with shyness or social anxiety. My best guess is that close to a third of the hundreds I've interviewed used alcohol this way, as a social lubricant and anxiety queller. Ironically, over time, alcohol exacerbates anxious feelings and causes more social problems, but we tend not to realize this until much later.

Sometimes using alcohol to socialize is just a lazy way to connect with others, a universal symbol for relaxation and fun. It can help people to interact superficially, clinking glasses and going through social contrivances without working very hard to extend themselves.

Quitting drinking can mean relearning social skills that were never fully developed to begin with, plus overcoming barriers of shyness and anxiety.

If you find small talk difficult, it can help to prepare a list of topics. Writing them down will let you remember them better, though I don't recommend pulling a paper out of your sleeve.

Earlier in the day, take five minutes to jot out three movies you've enjoyed, three books you'd recommend, and three lighthearted news stories (no politics, repeat, *no politics!*). Reread your notes before heading to a party. If you're stuck for conversation, you'll have a few standbys fresh in your mind.

Taking breaks can be very helpful if you struggle in groups. Check the surroundings for a quiet corner where you can touch base with online support from your smartphone or do a few breathing exercises to relax. In a pinch, the powder room works just fine as long as you don't settle in for too long.

Responding to others offering drinks can feel awkward and bring unwanted attention. Keep your glass full of your safe beverage, and you will be pestered less. Most people don't care what's in your glass; they're just trying to be thoughtful and friendly.

Dancing with a group is a great way to enjoy yourself and surprisingly fun when sober! I have a partner who doesn't love dancing, so I rely on friends who will dance in a circle. Group dancing lets people come and go without the awful awkwardness of individuals asking one another to dance and then feeling trapped together, wishing they'd planned even more small talk topics.

If you find that you just can't overcome the feelings of social anxiety at an event, be gentle with yourself. You may have misjudged your readiness to be at parties, or overbooked yourself that week. Be friendly, be polite, and leave. Go home and have a bath. Or go the movies and eat a bag of popcorn in the dark. You can call the host the next day and thank them for inviting you to their lovely event.

You're sober.

That's what matters.

Successful Socializing

If you take the time to prepare in advance by talking with your friends and your partner or support person, gather your mindset and consider boundaries, you'll find that socializing can go smoothly. It may seem like a lot of groundwork, but it's worth it. *You're* worth it.

It's easier to trust yourself and relax when you know you have all the bases covered.

Be sure to follow up afterward to show appreciation for other's support and tweak the plan for next time, if necessary.

Reflection Exercise:
What boundaries and guidelines do you choose for yourself in a social setting that includes alcohol?
What actions can you take to protect your recovery when you encounter triggers and discomfort?

Tool: Preparation

Advance communication with key people in your life can make everything go smoother. Be sure that others understand what is helpful and what isn't, like whether or not you prefer to be included in events that serve alcohol and how you plan to navigate those situations. Ask for what you need or provide it yourself, including transportation, personal space, beverages of choice, snacks, connection to support, and dancing shoes!

Tips for Friends and Family:

Take an interest in your friend's recovery and ask how you can best help them. Touch base with them periodically at social events and let them know that they're doing great.
A wink and a thumbs-up can go a long way.
Give sincere compliments to help boost confidence and tell them you're glad they're there.
Be patient if they don't seem quite themselves;
it takes time to find the new normal!
Follow up after a gathering to ask what went well
and what they might prefer to do differently next time.
Let them know you respect their decision to be sober
and appreciate that it can be difficult.

Wisdom from Sober Friends

> Take a break from people, make sure that you have friends that are supportive in your recovery. And remember, you don't have to do everything!

Catherine (20 months of sobriety)

" Have an exit plan! Bring your own drinks. Talk to friend/sponsor before you go and when you leave. Have a treat planned for when you get home – a bath, crappy TV, some ice cream, a good book. Whatever floats your boat.

Liz (14 months of sobriety)

" FOCUS on the different! Mornings are sure different sober! Holidays are actually physically demanding, and I am thankful to have more stamina, no hangovers and better sleep.

Laney (3+ years of sobriety)

" Try not to anything you don't want to do socially. Keep your own routine in place in December…yoga, healthy eating, reading. Find the parts of the holidays that bring meaning for you. Avoid the silliness and BS.

Margaret (5 1/2 years of sobriety)

" Sleep. Never back to back events. I choose entertainment over dinner parties. I like to schedule brunch or day time hikes or teas to celebrate with friends.

Diana (25 months of sobriety)

Stay connected to people in recovery.

Barry (427 days of sobriety)

 1. Stay engaged with your sober tribe online every day, either contributing or at least reading and responding.

2. Have your beautiful special drink in your hand at all times at parties and keep it over half full.

3. Go to parties early and leave early, unless you are having a blast.

4. Dance! Drink lots of water. Have fun!

5. Make sure to have pre-arranged a ride home for anytime you want. It might help to be the driver.

6. As the driver, make sure (ahead of time) the others are prepared to Uber home if you want to leave early.

7. Take care of yourself. Your recovery is the most important thing in your life. Treat it like you would treat chemo.

This means don't put too high of expectations on yourself. You might feel like Wonder Woman now that you're sober, but don't overdo it. Remember, it's a high-risk time for relapse. Don't overcommit yourself.

Marci (1064 days of sobriety)

I don't put myself in situations that I don't feel comfortable in. I always have a backup plan. I take sober friends with me if possible.

Sherri (5 3/4 years of sobriety)

In the very early days (30-60 days), I let the FOMO (fear of missing out) affect my mood, and I felt that I wanted a drink to be 'fun.' I've learned so much about myself on this journey and realized that my mood is controlled by me alone, and that's more fun than any hangover.

Kat (157 days of sobriety)

You don't have to go to every event you are invited to. Say no when you want to. Have a fridge full of non-alcoholic beverages to bring with you. Make up a 'cue' with your partner and ask your partner to [watch for it as a sign that] you need a little support.

Jan (1 year 10 months of sobriety)

Stay connected to your community/tribe. [It's] so easy to isolate, and that's when I'd get into trouble. Ask family for help. Accept help from friends.

Early to bed ... rest and balance.

Marie (900 days of sobriety)

I do more meetings, surround myself with recovery, and I bring my own drinks.

Julie (9.5 years of sobriety)

“ Surround your body (physically), mind and soul with all the lovely people you know that will uplift and support you. That is so big when you have people in your life to talk to, depend on, vent. If even online!

My sweet husband always makes sure I have a drink in hand and always has my back, which is such a help with the anxiety that comes with the pressure we put ourselves though when, in all actuality, nobody really notices. I think sometimes the ones that do notice are the ones that maybe need you to notice them, too.

Lucinda (590 days of sobriety)

“ Sober friends. Yoga. AA meetings. Prepare my expectations in advance. Arrive at events late and leave early when I want to. Accept that my sobriety is more important than people-pleasing. Boundaries are amazing to work with. And actually fun to practice when I put myself in a calm and open place, emotionally.

Elizabeth (23 months of sobriety)

NINE

A New Tradition

Word of the Year

Without a doubt, you will emerge from the intensity of the holiday season with new skills, insights, and tools. Whether it is your first sober year or your fiftieth, turning the page on another year stimulates reflection and planning.

A tradition that I was introduced to by recovery friends is choosing a 'Word of the Year' to serve as a guidepost and reminder of efforts to grow and heal.

Some choose a word that celebrates where they have been, while others choose a word to signify where they wish to go. It could be an emotion that you want to acknowledge, a trait you seek to embody, or a theme you'd like to embrace.

I admit that I was initially reluctant to join in on selecting a WOTY (word of the year).

I wanted hard, meaty tools in my recovery toolkit and felt that a lone word could not have the power to make the significant changes for which I strove.

Eventually, I was forced to choose a word when the concept was to be discussed on The Bubble Hour. I decided to be pragmatic and chose the word 'utilize.' (It occurs to me now that 'pragmatic' would be a great WOTY!)

Why 'utilize?' Well, I had spent so much energy learning new tools and concepts about recovery, and I wanted to hold myself account-able for actually *using* all of the new knowledge I'd acquired.

I'd discovered the importance of gratitude, forgiveness, reflection. I'd learned to value myself in new ways. I gained tools to lessen anxiety, grief, and ruminating thoughts.

It is one thing to have all of this information and another thing to use it.

Utilize.

My friend Ellie, creator and then a co-host of The Bubble Hour, made me a gorgeous bracelet sporting my practical WOTY. While other girls wore jewelry with inspiring inscriptions like 'breathe' or 'believe', I flaunted UTILIZE stamped in copper.

I belong to an online group that would occasionally have discussions about everyone's WOTY. I was pleasantly surprised to consider how my word choice nudged me to use my new tools and lessons more consistently.

Last year, realizing the power that a WOTY has to influence behaviour, I chose the word 'Create.' I'd dreamed of writing a novel and felt it was time to make a sincere effort. I also wanted to tap into other aspects of my creative side, like learning to paint.

Boy, did my word choice pay off! I fully embraced my passion for fiction writing and pursued the project with a new faith in myself. Now I have one novel completed plus another underway and several other writing projects in the works. I've joined writing groups and learned all about the process and business of creating, publishing and selling books. I also made jewelry, found online tutorials for watercolour projects, and have begun self-directed piano lessons.

By the time the year is over, the WOTY can become so ingrained in one's thinking that rather than casting it aside for a new word, it remains as a base layer to build upon with new words, concepts and ideas.

Embrace new traditions that grow and support your lifestyle of recovery.

Selecting a Word of The Year is a great start.

Reflection Exercise:
Look back on the growth and success you have experienced over the past year and consider how it feels to have come this far. What new tools and skills do you have that you are eager to utilize? What lessons and changes are still in process? How would you like to grow in the months to come? Hold these ideas together in your mind and see if a specific word emerges.

Tool: Word of the Year
A special word chosen as a guidepost to help direct the recovery goals and growth of the year ahead.

Tips for Friends and Family:
Take an interest in your loved one's Word of the Year. Ask why they've chosen it and what it means to them. Keep an eye out for small gifts that may include their special word; craft fairs and online markets often have various items to customize. A WOTY-related gift is a thoughtful way to commemorate a sober milestone.

Wisdom from Sober Friends

" [My WOTY is] Peace. I am so much more at peace with myself without alcohol in my life. Exponentially fewer regrets, no more hangovers.

Whenever I have the occasional thought it would be nice to pick up a drink I remind myself of the peace that I've created within and how drinking would destroy it.

Liz (14 months of sobriety)

" "Just This"

This means I will focus on one thing at a time.

Margaret (5 1/2 years of sobriety)

" I have never heard of 'Word of the Year,' but if I had to choose one, it would be 'pray.' I have learned to pray when I don't know what to do or what not to do. I pray for the willingness to be willing.

Sherri (5 3/4 years of sobriety)

" If I think of one now, it would be 'revival' because it has been a journey of soul searching, renewal, and rejuvenation combined to revive my spirit.

Kat (157 days of sobriety)

'Calm' was my word this year. It reminded me to be calm and breathe when I was a hot mess. I usually operate at about a 'seven' normally! So when I get amped up [to a 'ten'], it's not good. If I remind myself about my word, it brings instant results. I stop, calm myself, and breathe.

Jan (1 year 10 months of sobriety)

This year my word was 'Wholeheartedly.' This is how I want to live my life. It has definitely helped me in my decision making [and] it has helped me set boundaries as well.

Marie (900 days of sobriety)

Last year it was Believe. It helped me to believe in myself more.

Julie (9.5 years of sobriety)

'Open-hearted.' Be open to the possibilities. Stay curious. Explore my emotions and stay in the present.

Elizabeth (23 months of sobriety)

TEN

Your Holiday Toolkit

TERMS

Adaptive State:
Bringing forth the qualities demanded by a situation, while remaining true to ones self.

Addiction Transfer Behaviour:
The replacement of one addictive behaviour for another.

Codependent:
A person who is dependent on others to reflect self-identity and worth. It is sometimes called "other focussed" or "the disease of lost self."

Dopamine Downregulation:
The brain's adaptation to a dopamine response that results in a tolerance requiring higher and higher levels of stimulus to produce an effect.

Dopamine Response Cycle:
A process by which the brain becomes conditioned to seek specific dopamine-releasing behaviours.

Family of Origin:
The term used to describe the relationships surrounding an individual in childhood, typically parent(s) and sibling(s).

H.A.L.T. :
This acronym is often used as a reminder of four common triggers: feeling Hungry, Angry, Lonely, or Tired. If you find yourself craving a drink or feeling anxious, assess and address these triggers first.

Highest Self:
Although his term may be used differently in certain religious or spiritual practices, "Highest Self" as used within these pages refers to the mindset of reflective engagement in accordance with the values held dear; an intentional best effort to utilize all skills and lessons to the best of one's current ability.

Imposter Syndrome:
The inward feeling of being a fraud despite outward evidence of competence and success.

Natural State:
How one naturally behaves without adapting to external demands.

Normie:
A person who drinks alcohol without compulsion or addiction, or a "normal" drinker.

Process Addiction:
Pleasure-inducing behaviours that become obsessive and compulsive, without the presence of an addictive substance. These behaviours can include gambling, sex, pornography, eating, shopping, exercising, computer games or internet use.

Replacement Behaviours:
New patterns that emerge to replace drinking, most effective when a dopamine response is solicited.

Stages of Change:
Pre-contemplative, Contemplative, Preparation, Action, and Maintenance.

THE REFLECTION EXERCISES

Chapter 1: The Most Wonderful Time of the Year

Reflection Exercise:

Spend some quiet time considering how you genuinely feel about the holiday season. What pleases you, and what makes you anxious? What do you look forward to, and what do you dread?

Chapter 2: Expectations

Reflection Exercise:

What standards and virtues do you value and wish to practice at all times? What is inside your bubble with you wherever you go? What aspects of your own conduct will you use as a measure of success?

Chapter 3: The Invites

Reflection Exercise:

Stand before a mirror and practice speaking the responses to typical pressure tactics as suggested above.

The more you practice saying such phrases, the easier it is to recall them for use in real-time:

- "That's sweet of you to say, but I'm sure you'll all have a great time."

- "I understand. Sorry I can't make it."
- "Have fun. We will get everyone together another time."
- "It doesn't work for me this year, but thank you for the invite."

Chapter 4: Family Gatherings

Reflection Exercise:

Write a list of any coping roles, masks, or identities you find yourself slipping into in situations with family members. These may relate to your place in the birth (such as the responsible eldest or infantilized youngest) or your role within the family dynamic (jester, scapegoat, or rebel, for example).

It's possible to have more than one such role or masks.

Consider the ways that these identities may reflect true aspects of yourself, how they are exaggerations or entirely false, and what purpose they serve.

Next, write what it feels like to be your "Highest Self," referring to times in which you are not wearing a mask or playing a role but intentionally utilizing all of your skills, values, and awareness to the best of your ability.

Finally, recall situations in which each various mask was used, then imagine the same situations with you as your "Highest Self."

Chapter 5: Hosting an Event

Reflection Exercise:

Imagine the special accommodations you would make for a sober person attending an event at your home. Write out all of the ways you would support a friend in recovery at your party, dinner, or gathering.

These are the things you should do for yourself as the host of the event. Be as kind and thoughtful towards yourself as you are to others.

Chapter 6: Replacement vs. Transfer

Reflection Exercise:

Think about the activities you enjoy that have the potential to become process addictions. Consider some guidelines for yourself to help keep these activities in check. For example, make a budget for unnecessary shopping, use the settings on electronic devices to monitor and limit the amount of time spent on games or social media, and write out any red flags you can be watchful for regarding potentially problematic pastimes.

Be especially mindful that the holiday season emphasizes extra spending and eating.

Chapter 7: Work Obligations

Reflection Exercise:

Make a list of goals to achieve at work-related functions: networking, volunteer requirements, bid on the silent auction, hear the guest speaker, say hello to coworkers' family members, etc.

Make an effort to accomplish this list of goals within the first hour of the event and then give yourself permission to leave the moment you decide it is time, knowing that you have done your duty by attending. If you are comfortable and are enjoying yourself, then you can stay as long as you like!

Chapter 8: Socializing

Reflection Exercise:

What boundaries and guidelines do you choose for yourself in a social setting that includes alcohol? What actions can you take to protect your recovery when you encounter triggers and discomfort?

Chapter 9: A New Tradition

Reflection Exercise:

Look back on the growth and success you have experienced over the past year and consider how it feels to have come this far. What new tools and skills do you have that you are eager to utilize? What lessons and changes are still in process? How would you like to grow in the months to come?

Hold these ideas together in your mind and see if a specific word emerges.

THE TOOLS

Chapter 1 Tool: Willingness

It's essential to be willing to do things differently if you would like to see change. Give yourself permission to question the usual way of doing things and stand by any decisions you make in your own best interest.

Chapter 2 Tool: Discernment

Learn to identify the things you assume are "normal" that are really expectations. Letting go of expectations will reduce negative feelings of resentment that undermine recovery.

Chapter 3 Tool: Take alongs

As you choose which invitations to accept, prepare the 'take alongs' you will need for each event. A smartphone preloaded with links to message boards, recovery pages, and support groups; a snack and beverage; car keys or cab fare; a thank you gift for the host.

Chapter 4 Tool: Highest Self Mindset

A conscious effort to draw together all skills, values and awareness in harmony with your deepest, truest, best self. This mindset can be visualized as being encased around you in a bubble to protect and contain these qualities, and through which everything projected is a reflection of the values within. It is from this place that one can ask the question "is that true" as a means to challenge old beliefs and expectations.

Chapter 5 Tool: Recovery Nest

Choose a place in your home (or the location of the event to be hosted) that can serve as your own personal getaway. It should have privacy and a comfortable place to sit or lay down and be away from the area where guests will be. Add items that can support short time-outs in this space as a way to reset physically and emotionally: a meditation cushion, headphones and a short meditation guide, snacks, and a bottle of water. Include a timer, which will allow you to relax more deeply without worry that you will fall asleep or stay too long. Even if you don't use this hideaway during your event, just knowing it's available to you can be a comfort.

Chapter 6 Tool: Replacement Behaviours

Healthy alternatives to an addictive behaviour or substance that help to bring comfort while supporting recovery.

Chapter 7 Tool: Delayed Gratification

Have a planned reward to look forward to immediately after the event: a lovely bath, a new book, a sweet treat. Celebrate your successful navigation of the evening by coming home to a pre-planned treat.

Chapter 8 Tool: Preparation

Advance communication with key people in your life can make everything go smoother. Be sure that others understand what is helpful and what isn't, like whether or not you prefer to be included in events that serve alcohol and how you plan to navigate those situations. Ask for what you need or provide it yourself, including transportation, personal space, beverages of choice, snacks, connection to support, and dancing shoes!

Chapter 9 Tool: Word of the Year

A special word chosen as a guidepost to help direct the recovery goals and growth of the year ahead.

TIPS FOR FRIENDS AND FAMILY

Chapter 1: The Most Wonderful Time of the Year

Tips for Friends and Family:

Support your loved one in recovery by being open to change. Understand that it can be difficult for them to live life differently if everything around them stays the same. Begin with a private conversation to ask if there is anything special you can do to support their recovery during holiday events. If they share with you that some aspect of the usual tradition is challenging for them, listen without judgement and do not take offence. It is not a criticism of you or the way you do things. Consider new ways of doing things and be willing to compromise.

Chapter 2: Expectations

Tips for Friends and Family:

Think about the ways that you and your loved one in recovery may hold unspoken expectations for one another regarding holiday events and traditions. Have a discussion to explore these expectations and decide if they are real or perceived, fair and necessary, and consider ways that you can release one another from them. Swap expectations for agreed-upon responsibilities and boundaries for all family members, then be patient as dynamics shift.

Chapter 3: The Invites

Tips for Friends and Family:

Understand that if your loved one declines an invitation, it's not a rejection of you but a decision to avoid circumstances that may not feel right for them.

Suggest alternatives or adjust plans to include a limited timeframe that better suits them, or release them from the obligation altogether.

The acceptance or decline of invitations may change from year to year as their recovery evolves, so do continue to extend invitations, even if declined in the past.

Do not assume that a person in recovery will not want to attend an event. It may feel considerate to leave them off of the guestlist for an event that will include alcohol, but usually, that is more hurtful than helpful. Leave that decision up to them.

Do consider creating new events or parts of events that are alcohol-free, such as a morning or afternoon meetup.

Focus on ways to spend time together doing activities as an alternative to the usual gatherings focussed solely on food and alcohol.

Chapter 4: Family Gatherings

Tips for Friends and Family:

Provide a quiet space removed from the crowd that your loved one in recovery can slip off to if they should need a break or time alone. Let them know that this place is available for them, if they wish to use it.

You might even go the extra mile of adding some bottles of water, a few snacks, a blanket, or other comforts.

Just providing this place is an act of support and love, so don't be offended or disappointed if it isn't used.

Have a variety of alcohol-free choices on hand. Be sure they are clearly labelled and openly available. Remember that your loved one may still be discovering what they enjoy, so even if the choices you supply don't appeal to them now, they might be a new favourite in the future.

Especially in early recovery, each outing can be different as new boundaries and coping skills are explored, so be flexible.

Call to follow up after events and discuss possible adjustments for next time.

Respect recovery, it isn't easy.

Meet them where they are at today.

Chapter 5: Hosting an Event

Tips for Friends and Family:

Do not make assumptions about whether an event hosted by a person in recovery will or will not involve alcohol. The best plan is to discuss this in advance and respect their boundaries and wishes. Some sober hosts have alcohol-free homes, some are comfortable with other people bringing their own alcohol as long as they take it home again afterwards, and some will make full accommodation for guests who wish to drink.

Offer to help with the event by bringing food or helping with preparations. If alcohol is present, offer to look after the serving and clean up of alcoholic drinks. Often the handling of used wine glasses can be just as triggering as pouring drinks, so rinse out glassware and empty bottles. Gather up leftover alcohol and remove it after the event (unless otherwise requested).

Compliment the host on the food and decorations. Show gratitude for their efforts.

Offer to cover the hosting duties for a few minutes here and there to allow them to take a break if needed.

Remember to bring the host a thank you gift that isn't a bottle of wine! Ideas include flowers, a candle, a book, soap or lotion, chocolates, decorative hand towels or dishcloths.

Chapter 6: Replacement vs. Transfer

Tips for Friends and Family:

Keep an eye out for warning signs of addiction transfer, such as prolonged isolation and avoidance of regular responsibilities in favour of an activity with process addiction potential. While accusations or advice are not helpful, do voice observations neutrally and ask questions to help spark awareness. Communicate simply:

"I notice you're doing a lot of (activity). How is that going for you?"

Since change begins with awareness (see *Stages of Change* in Chapter 10: Terms), raising your concerns can incite the process of change.

Remember that activities with the potential to become process addictions can also be effective short-term substitutions for the original addiction. Encourage and support your loved one as they pursue recovery-related activities (meetings or groups, therapy, consuming recovery materials, working with a coach, physical activity and self-care) that will contribute to their overall understanding and healing of the issues underlying the addiction. As this work progresses, other symptoms like process addictions can slowly resolve.

Chapter 7: Work Obligations

Tips for Friends and Family:

If you are accompanying a sober friend or family member to a work event, be sure to keep an eye on their glass and help them keep it filled with a safe choice of their choosing. Be supportive without making a show of it to others. Either plan to leave whenever they are ready or arrange to have separate transportation if it is likely that you may want to stay longer. Discuss this in advance and agree on options so that the evening can unfold smoothly.

Chapter 8: Socializing

Tips for Friends and Family:

Take an interest in your friend's recovery and ask how you can best help them. Touch base with them periodically at social events and let them know that they're doing great.

A wink and a thumbs-up can go a long way.

Give sincere compliments to help boost confidence and tell them you're glad they're there.

Be patient if they don't seem quite themselves; it takes time to find the new normal!

Follow up after a gathering to ask what went well and what they might prefer to do differently next time. Let them know you respect their decision to be sober and appreciate that it can be difficult.

Chapter 9: A New Tradition

Tips for Friends and Family:

Take an interest in your loved one's Word of the Year. Ask why they've chosen it and what it means to them. Keep an eye out for small gifts that may include their special word; craft fairs and online markets often have various items to customize. A WOTY-related gift is a thoughtful way to commemorate a sober milestone.

Author's Notes

This book is a collection of helpful information gathered from eight years worth of of UnPickled blog posts and The Bubble Hour podcast episodes.

I'm beyond grateful to the many people online and in-person who took the time to share their recovery stories and insights. They've shaped my growth with their wisdom and kindness.

I hold up this book as a mirror of the goodness I see in the recovery world.

I hope it helps to reinforce your strengths and sparks some new ideas, too.

I wish you all the best over the holidays and always.

As ever my friends,
Take good care.

Jean
www.jeanmccarthy.ca